The **TEENAGE MUTANT NINJA TURTLES**®

Pizza Cookbook

The
TEENAGE MUTANT NINJA
TURTLES®

Pizza Cookbook

Written by **PEGGY PAUL CASELLA**

Photography by **ALBERT YEE**

INSIGHT ⓘ EDITIONS

SAN RAFAEL · LOS ANGELES · LONDON

CONTENTS

Old School

New School

Masked Mutations

Sweet, Dude!

DID YOU KNOW, BRO?
CREATED BY KEVIN EASTMAN AND PETER LAIRD, THE TEENAGE MUTANT NINJA TURTLES STARTED OUT AS A BLACK-AND-WHITE COMIC BOOK IN 1984.

INTRODUCTION

After an epic (and totally triumphant) battle with Bebop, Rocksteady, and the rest of Shredder's gang, there's nothing the Teenage Mutant Ninja Turtles enjoy more than kicking back in their lair with a stack of piping-hot, cheesy pizzas. The only thing better is if those pizzas are homemade, baked by Michelangelo in one of Donny's souped-up ovens.

In this book, you'll find all of the Turtles' go-to recipes, along with tips and tricks to master the art of pizza-making at home—whether you're a novice or a culinary ninja! You can buy your own dough and sauce, or you can make them from scratch (pages 17–27). Don't have a fancy baking stone? No problemo! All you really need is a heavy-duty, rimmed baking sheet and a few other basic kitchen tools.

If you're like Mikey, and you want your pizzas to walk on the wild side, there's a whole chapter just for you. Try the awesome Mac Attack (page 55), Pepperoni and Sweet Pickle Pie (page 79), and the Breakfast Pie (page 57). More of a traditionalist? Head over to the Old School section to find old familiars such as New York–Style Pepperoni Pizza (page 33), Snowmageddon (page 40), and Sausage and Pepper POW! (page 39). Then shake up your meal routine with Pizza Potstickers (page 85), Raph's Waffles (page 96), or one of the other twisted Masked Mutations. And what's for dessert, you ask? More pizza, of course! Check out the last chapter for tasty treats such as New York Cheesecake Pizza (page 113), Gimme S'mores! pizza (page 117), and Casey's Cookies (page 107).

Are you hungry yet? Then come on, *compadres*—let's get cooking!

HEALTHY SWAPS AND COOKING TIPS

In order to keep his students in crime-fighting shape, Master Splinter has developed some seriously stealthy mealtime moves, slipping extra veggies onto their plates when the Turtles aren't looking, swapping their regular pizza crust for a tasty whole-wheat version (page 18), and reducing the amounts of salt, oil, and fat when it's his turn to cook. He was worried at first that they'd catch on and revolt against his health-conscious ways, but when Michelangelo started to request extra broccoli on his classic pepperoni pie, Splinter knew he'd won them over. Check out the "Lighten It Up, Dude!" callouts throughout the book for ways to cut down on fat and up the nutritional benefits of specific recipes. And follow these ten simple rules to make healthy cooking a part of your everyday routine:

1. Cut down on oil. Whenever a recipe calls for oil, try reducing the amount by a teaspoon or tablespoon. Only use as much as you need to keep the food from sticking to the pan.
2. Season with herbs, spices, and citrus. According to the American Heart Association, high amounts of sodium can make your body hold onto water, which may affect your blood pressure and heart health. So the next time you feel like reaching for the saltshaker, try a spritz of lemon or lime instead, or a sprinkle of dried herbs or spices. These salt-free seasonings will add a satisfying flavor boost to any recipe, with the added benefit of extra nutrition.

3. Go whole grain. Whole-wheat flour contains way more dietary fiber and essential vitamins and minerals than refined white flour. If you're not sure you'll like the taste of 100 percent whole-wheat pizza crust, ease yourself in by making One-Hour Dough (page 19) or Overnight Dough (page 17) with one-third or half whole-wheat flour.

4. Think more veggies and fruits, less dairy and meat. The USDA recommends that you fill half of your plate with vegetables and fruits at every meal, then add a generous amount of whole grains, a serving of lean protein that fills no more than one quarter of the plate, and a modest amount of dairy on the side. This plate analogy also works well on pizza. Just amp up the amounts of whole, fresh ingredients and show restraint when adding meat and cheese toppings. Or go vegetarian by swapping out the meat for cooked, crumbled tofu.

5. Choose low-fat dairy options. If a recipe calls for ricotta, heavy cream, or milk, consider using a low-fat option if available.

6. Steam, roast, grill, or sauté—don't fry. Some cooking techniques are healthier than others. Whenever a recipe calls for precooked ingredients, use methods such as steaming, poaching, grilling, roasting, and sautéing, which all require much less oil or fat than frying, and resist the urge to season with extra salt.

7. Use natural sweeteners. Instead of refined sugar, opt for honey or pure maple syrup and sprinkle in some vanilla extract, cinnamon, or other spices to satisfy your taste buds.

8. Hold the sauce. If you're tempted to douse your pizza with hot sauce, ranch dressing, or some other condiment or sauce, make sure you taste a slice before adding any extras. These flavor enhancers are usually not needed, and they add more fat and empty calories to your meal.

9. Portion it out. If you leave half a pizza on the counter while you eat dinner, it'll be much more tempting to go back for seconds or thirds. Instead, once you fill everyone's dinner plate, wrap the rest in foil for tomorrow and put it right in the refrigerator. Out of sight, out of mind.

10. Slow down. It's never good to act in haste, and that goes for eating as much as it does for ninja training. By taking the time to chew your food completely, you allow your body to absorb more nutrients, and you reduce your risk of overeating, which can lead to weight gain and other health issues.

KITCHEN-NINJA TRAINING

Like the ancient art of ninjutsu, homemade pizza also takes time and practice. There are techniques to master—making the dough (pages 17–19), stretching or rolling it out (page 14), and whipping up cooked and raw sauces (pages 21–27)—and, of course, there are special weapons that will help bring your moves to the next level. In this chapter, you'll learn the basic pillars of pizza-making, including a list of essential tools and ingredients, three different dough recipes, and basic sauces and toppings. Armed with these skills and simple recipes, there's no limit to the pizzas you can create.

COOKING WITH NINJAS IN TRAINING

Pizza is an awesome way to get kids of all ages involved in the kitchen. Preschoolers can help press out the dough, stir and spread on the sauce, and put the toppings on the pizza before baking. School-age kids can learn basic cooking moves, prep the ingredients using kid-safe knives and scissors, and test their reading and math skills by trying to follow the recipe directions. Teens can hone their kitchen-ninja craft with more difficult tasks, such as making the dough, sauces, and other cooked ingredients. With supervision, they can also help transfer the pizzas to and from the oven.

For best results, have a few snacks on hand to keep hunger at bay while you cook and make sure everyone knows the rules of the kitchen: Wash your hands before and in between all tasks, pay attention to what you're doing at all times, don't touch sharp knives or oven and stove knobs, keep a safe distance from the hot oven, and use potholders whenever you take anything out of the oven or off the hot stove.

WHAT YOU NEED TO MAKE PIZZA AT HOME

You don't need a kitchen tricked out with gadgets from Donnie's lab to make homemade pizza, but there are some cool tools that will make things easier. Here are the basics, plus some secret weapons and go-to ingredients to keep on hand—because you never know when a dangerous pizza craving may strike.

INGREDIENTS FOR SUCCESS

- Canned, whole, peeled tomatoes
- Dried herbs
- Fine sea salt
- Black pepper
- Instant/quick-rise yeast
- Sugar
- Bread flour
- Cheeses
- Vegetables
- Pickled veggies
- Cured meats (bacon, prosciutto, pepperoni)

ESSENTIAL TOOLS

- Large mixing bowls
- Sturdy wooden spoon
- Whisk
- Dry and wet measuring cups and spoons
- Plastic wrap
- Clean kitchen towels
- Rolling pin
- Box grater
- At least one heavy-duty rimmed baking sheet (aka a half sheet pan)
- Large cutting board
- Pizza cutter

SECRET WEAPONS

- Food processor
- Electric mixer
- Baking stone or steel
- Pizza peel
- 12-inch pizza pan
- Garlic press
- Herb stripper
- Pastry brush
- Assorted prep bowls or ramekins
- Mandoline slicer
- Fresh herbs
- Pizza cutter

NINJA MASTER TECHNIQUES

STRETCHING OR ROLLING OUT THE DOUGH

To roll or not to roll? It's simply a matter of taste. If you like an airy pizza crust with bubbles that char up a little in the oven, then you'll want to stretch it by hand. If you like a denser, more uniform crust, then you'll want to flatten it out with a rolling pin before topping.

TO STRETCH YOUR DOUGH BY HAND

1. Place the dough ball on a well-floured work surface. Flour your hands and use your palm to flatten the dough slightly into a small, thick disk.

2. Then, starting in the center, use your fingertips to push the dough outward, spreading your fingers to expand the size of the disk.

3. Finally, pick up the disk of dough, draping it over your two fists. Gently move your fists apart under the dough, switching direction and rotating the dough until you have a 12-inch square or circle.

TO ROLL OUT YOUR DOUGH

1. Place the dough ball on a well-floured work surface. Flour a rolling pin.

2. Press down on the dough with the rolling pin and roll it slowly back and forth, rotating the dough after every roll or two until you have a 12-inch square or circle. If the dough keeps shrinking as you roll it out, stop rolling and let it rest on the counter for 10 to 15 minutes, then try again.

USING A PIZZA PEEL & BAKING STEEL/STONE

You don't need a baking stone or steel to make awesome pizza at home, but it will help you replicate the extra-crispy crust from your favorite pizzeria's wood-burning oven. First, look for a large (at least 14-inch) square or rectangular stone or steel. Circular ones may look pretty, but their smaller surface areas make for more difficult targets when you're transferring the topped pizza from the peel to the oven. Then, make sure you also buy yourself a pizza peel. The biggest challenge is getting the topped pizza onto the hot stone, and these large, long-handled wooden or metal paddles are the best tools for the job.

FOLLOW THESE STEPS

1. Place your baking stone or steel in the middle of the oven while it's off, then preheat to the temperature designated in the recipe.

2. Dust your pizza peel with cornmeal or flour, and place the stretched or rolled-out dough on top.

3. Pile on the toppings.

4. Give the peel a little shake. If the pizza doesn't move, tuck more cornmeal or flour underneath it and shake again. If it still doesn't move, slide a flat spatula between the dough and the peel to loosen it up a bit.

5. Open the oven door. Holding the handle tightly, lower the tip of the peel so it touches toward the back of the hot stone or steel. Either shimmy or jerk the pizza peel toward you until the pizza slides onto the stone or steel.

6. Bake as directed in the recipe.

7. Slide the peel under the finished pizza to retrieve it from the oven.

GRILLING PIZZA

The crispiest pizza crusts come from wood-fired ovens, which can get smokin' hot—up to 800°F! But you don't need to build a radical contraption to achieve crust nirvana at home. (Sorry, Donatello.) A gas or charcoal grill will do the trick. Just follow these easy steps.

Special Tools: Long-handled brush, long-handled tongs, pizza peel or two long-handled spatulas

1. Preheat your grill to high heat with the lid on.

2. While the grill heats up, prep all your ingredients and arrange them within arm's reach of your grill.

3. Roll out your dough and brush it on one side with olive oil.

4. Carefully plop the dough, oiled side down, onto the hot grill grate. Brush some oil on top of the dough and cover the grill. Cook for about 2 minutes or until the dough is just set and has golden brown grill marks on the bottom.

5. Using long-handled tongs, immediately flip the dough. Top it with cheese and the rest of the ingredients. Cover the grill and cook for another 3 minutes or until the cheese is melted and the bottom of the crust is crispy with golden brown grill marks.

6. Quickly remove the pizza from the grill using a pizza peel or two large spatulas. Slice and enjoy!

OVERNIGHT DOUGH

MAKES 2 POUNDS OF DOUGH

A favorite recipes of the Turtles, this longer-ferment dough is perfectly flavored and bakes up amazingly light on the inside and crispy on the outside. **TIMING HINT:** Mix the dough at 9 or 10 p.m. to make pizza for dinner the next day. Timing. Patience. Fermentation. Do these bros know a lot about dough or what?

INGREDIENTS

3 ³/₄ cups bread flour

¹/₄ teaspoon active dry or instant yeast

2 teaspoons fine sea salt

1 teaspoon sugar

1 ¹/₂ cups cold water

1 tablespoon extra-virgin olive oil

INSTRUCTIONS

1. In a large bowl, whisk together the flour, yeast, salt, and sugar.

2. Add the water and oil and mix with your hands or a wooden spoon until all of the flour is incorporated. The dough will be sticky.

3. Cover the bowl with plastic wrap and let it rise at room temperature for 18 to 20 hours or until it has more than doubled in volume.

4. Scrape the dough out onto a floured work surface and use a knife or scraper to divide it in half.*

5. Shape each piece of dough by folding its four sides under toward the center, then forming it into a ball. If the dough feels sticky, dust it with flour.

6. Cover the formed dough balls with a damp kitchen towel and let them rest for 30 minutes or up to 3 hours before using. (Or, if you're not making pizza right away, wrap the balls loosely with plastic wrap and store them in the refrigerator for up to 3 days.)

7. Roll or stretch out the dough, add desired toppings, and bake.

* If you're planning to make one large baking sheet pizza, do not divide the dough in half. Simply plop the whole thing onto a heavy-duty rimmed baking sheet and stretch it out.

WHOLE-WHEAT PIZZA DOUGH

MAKES 2 POUNDS OF DOUGH

A ninja uses his mind as well as his body, and Master Splinter knows that healthy food is brain food. He makes sure his sons get a kick of extra nutrition by swapping their regular pizzas for whole wheat every now and then.

INGREDIENTS

3 ½ cups whole-wheat flour

1 teaspoon fine sea salt

1 teaspoon sugar

One ¼-ounce package instant or rapid-rise dry yeast

1 tablespoon honey

1 ½ cups warm water

1 tablespoon extra-virgin olive oil, plus more for coating

INSTRUCTIONS

MIXING BY HAND:

1. In a large bowl, stir together the flour, salt, sugar, and yeast with a wooden spoon.

2. Dissolve the honey in the warm water and pour this mixture over the flour, along with the olive oil.

3. Mix for at least 30 seconds with the wooden spoon or your hands until the dough just comes together into a ball and pulls away from the sides of the bowl. Proceed onto step 4 below.

USING A FOOD PROCESSOR (WITH DOUGH BLADE) OR ELECTRIC MIXER (WITH DOUGH HOOK):

1. In the bowl of a food processor or electric mixer, combine the flour, salt, sugar, and yeast.

2. Dissolve the honey in the warm water. With the machine running on dough speed (food processor) or medium (electric mixer), stream in the honey water, followed by the olive oil.

3. Keep mixing the dough for 30 seconds after it comes together into a ball and pulls away from the sides of the bowl. Transfer the dough to a floured work surface and knead until it's smooth and no longer sticky, adding more flour as necessary.

4. Rub the inside of a large, clean bowl liberally with olive oil. Place the dough ball in the oiled bowl and turn it to coat the entire ball in oil. Cover the bowl with plastic wrap and let the dough rise in a warm place for 45 minutes to 1 hour.* (It should double in size.)

5. After the dough is finished rising, punch it down, divide it into two equal pieces, and shape each piece into a ball.** Cover the dough balls with a damp kitchen towel and let them rest for at least 10 minutes or up to 1 hour. (Or, if you're not making pizza right away, wrap the balls loosely with plastic wrap and store them in the refrigerator for up to 3 days.)

6. Roll or stretch out the dough, add desired toppings, and bake.

*If you have the time, let the dough rise for an additional hour for a lighter, airier pizza crust.
**If you're planning to make one large baking sheet pizza, do not divide the dough in half. Simply plop the whole thing onto a heavy-duty, rimmed baking sheet and stretch it out.

ONE-HOUR PIZZA DOUGH

MAKES 2 POUNDS OF DOUGH

Transform any old weeknight into a fabuloso pizza night! Just stir it all together, preheat the oven, and kick back. In an hour, the dough will be ready to roll.

INGREDIENTS

3 1/3 cups bread flour

1 1/2 teaspoons salt

1 teaspoon sugar

One 1/4-ounce package instant or rapid-rise dry yeast

1 1/4 to 1 1/2 cups warm water

Extra-virgin olive oil

Lighten It Up, **DUDE!** USE WHOLE-WHEAT PIZZA DOUGH (PAGE 18) AND LOW-FAT MOZZARELLA.

INSTRUCTIONS

MIXING BY HAND:

1. In a large bowl, stir together the flour, salt, sugar, and yeast with a wooden spoon.

2. Pour in the water and mix for at least 30 seconds with the wooden spoon or your hands, until the dough just starts to come together into a ball and pulls away from the sides of the bowl. (If the dough looks too dry and isn't coming together, mix in a little more water, 1 teaspoon at a time.) Proceed onto step 3 below.

USING A FOOD PROCESSOR (WITH DOUGH BLADE) OR ELECTRIC MIXER (WITH DOUGH HOOK):

1. In the bowl of a food processor or electric mixer, combine the flour, salt, sugar, and yeast. With the machine running on dough speed (food processor) or medium (electric mixer), stream in the water.

2. Keep processing/mixing the dough for 30 seconds after it comes together into a ball and pulls away from the sides of the bowl. (If the dough looks too dry and isn't coming together, mix in a little more water, 1 teaspoon at a time.) Transfer the dough to a lightly floured work surface and knead until it's smooth and no longer sticky, adding a little more flour if needed.

3. Rub the inside of a large, clean bowl liberally with olive oil. Place the dough ball in the oiled bowl and turn it to coat the entire ball in oil. Cover the bowl with plastic wrap and let the dough rise in a warm place for 45 minutes to 1 hour.* (It should double in size.)

4. After the dough has finished rising, punch it down, divide it into two equal pieces, and shape each piece into a ball.**

5. Cover the dough balls with a damp kitchen towel and let them rest for at least 10 minutes or up to 1 hour. (Or, if you're not making pizza right away, wrap the balls loosely with plastic wrap and store them in the refrigerator for up to 3 days.)

6. Roll or stretch out the dough, add desired toppings, and bake.

*This recipe is meant for easy weeknight cooking, but if you have the time, let the dough rise for an extra hour for a lighter, airier pizza crust.

**If you're planning to make one large baking sheet pizza, do not divide the dough in half. Simply plop the whole thing onto a heavy-duty, rimmed baking sheet and stretch it out.

NO-COOK TOMATO SAUCE

MAKES ABOUT 3 ¼ CUPS

Mikey keeps olive oil, garlic, and a can or two of whole, peeled tomatoes in the Turtle Lair kitchen at all times, so he's always ready to whip up a homemade pizza on the fly. This zippy, fresh sauce is his favorite for the Old-School Italian pizza (page 34), Sausage and Pepper POW! (page 39), and for dipping Pizza Potstickers (page 85).

INGREDIENTS

One 28-ounce can whole, peeled tomatoes, drained

2 garlic cloves, pressed or grated

1 teaspoon fine sea salt

2 tablespoons extra-virgin olive oil

Freshly ground black pepper

INSTRUCTIONS

1. Dump the tomatoes into the bowl of a food processor and pulse a few times until they are broken down into a chunky sauce consistency. (Alternatively, dump them into a large bowl and crush them with a potato masher.)

2. Transfer the crushed tomatoes to a medium bowl and add the garlic, salt, olive oil, and a grind or two of black pepper.

3. Let the sauce marinate for about 15 minutes before using. Store any extra sauce in an airtight container in the refrigerator for up to 4 days or in the freezer for up to 6 months.

NEW YORK-STYLE PIZZA SAUCE

MAKES 2 CUPS

This thick, cooked-down sauce makes a great base for all sorts of topping combinations. (Yes, even Michelangelo's favorites.) In the summer, try subbing in chopped, vine-ripened tomatoes, and swap the oregano for finely chopped fresh basil.

INGREDIENTS

One 28-ounce can whole, peeled tomatoes

1 tablespoon extra-virgin olive oil

1 tablespoon unsalted butter

¼ cup finely diced yellow onion

1 large garlic clove, minced or pressed

1 tablespoon finely chopped fresh oregano (or 1 teaspoon dried)

1 teaspoon sugar

½ teaspoon fine sea salt

Freshly ground black pepper

INSTRUCTIONS

1. Dump the tomatoes and their juices into a large, deep bowl and squish the tomatoes with your hands until all of them are crushed into small pieces.

2. Heat the oil and butter in a medium saucepan over medium heat. When the butter is completely melted, add the onion. Cook for 3 to 5 minutes or until soft, and then add the garlic and cook for 30 seconds longer, just until fragrant.

3. Pour the crushed tomatoes into the pan, along with the oregano, sugar, salt, and a few grinds of pepper. Stir well.

4. Reduce the heat to low and simmer, partially covered, for 1 hour or until the sauce reaches the desired consistency.

5. Remove the pan from the heat and let the sauce come to room temperature before using.

DID YOU KNOW, BRO?

THE FIRST LICENSE TO MAKE AND SELL PIZZA IN THE UNITED STATES WAS ISSUED IN 1905 TO GENNARO LOMBARDI, WHO OWNED A PIZZA SHOP ON SPRING STREET IN NEW YORK CITY. IT IS OPEN TO THIS DAY IF YOU'RE EVER IN NEW YORK AND WANT TO PAY HOMAGE TO PIZZA HISTORY!

WHITE PIZZA SAUCE

MAKES ABOUT 1 CUP

When you want a pizza that's cheesy to the max, this sauce does the job. Get in touch with your inner Donatello and experiment with different chopped fresh herbs, dried spices, or even hot sauce.

INGREDIENTS

2 tablespoons unsalted butter

3 large garlic cloves, pressed or grated

2 tablespoons all-purpose flour

1 cup whole or reduced fat milk

¼ teaspoon salt

Freshly ground black pepper

¼ cup grated Parmesan cheese

INSTRUCTIONS

1. Melt the butter in a small saucepan over medium heat.

2. When it stops foaming, add the garlic. Cook for 30 seconds, and then sprinkle in the flour. Cook for 1 to 2 minutes longer, whisking constantly.

3. Add the milk to the saucepan in a slow stream while you continue whisking with the other hand.

4. Add the salt and a grind or two of pepper. Cook for 5 minutes or until the sauce has thickened to your liking.

5. Remove the pan from the heat and stir in the cheese. Use immediately or store it in an airtight container in the refrigerator for up to 3 days.

OLIVE TAPENADE

MAKES ABOUT 1 CUP

Master Splinter taught his sons the word *umami*. It's a Japanese term for that earthy, savory flavor found in foods like olives and mushrooms. Whenever the umami craving hits hard, the brothers buzz up a batch of tapenade in the food processor Donatello made out of a busted mouser robot! Tapenade is killer on pasta and as a dip with crackers and cheese, but of course the Turtles like it best on pizza.

INGREDIENTS

2 cups pitted kalamata or other black olives

2 anchovy fillets, packed in oil

1 garlic clove, pressed or grated

$1/4$ cup fresh flat-leaf parsley leaves

1 tablespoon capers

1 tablespoon freshly squeezed orange juice

$1/2$ teaspoon dried thyme

3 tablespoons extra-virgin olive oil

Freshly ground black pepper

INSTRUCTIONS

1. Combine all the ingredients except the black pepper in a food processor or blender and mix them all together until everything is minced and the mixture is uniform in color.

2. Season with black pepper to taste.

3. Store any extra tapenade in an airtight container in the refrigerator for up to 1 week.

ANY-HERB PESTO

MAKES ABOUT 1 CUP

Pesto is usually made with basil, but it's just as good with any other fresh, leafy herb. Try parsley, chives, mint, arugula, or even kale—or a mix. If you don't have Raph's super-sharp *sai* to chop up the leaves, a food processor will have to do!

INGREDIENTS

- **3 packed cups roughly chopped fresh leafy herbs or greens**
- **¼ cup pine nuts, chopped almonds, walnuts, pistachios, or any other nut you like**
- **¾ cup freshly grated Parmesan cheese**
- **1 large garlic clove**
- **1 ½ teaspoons freshly squeezed lemon juice**
- **⅛ teaspoon fine sea salt**
- **¼ cup extra-virgin olive oil**

INSTRUCTIONS

1. In a food processor, pulse all the ingredients except for the oil until well combined and very finely chopped.

2. With the motor running, stream in the oil and process until smooth.

3. Taste and add more salt and/or lemon juice as desired. (But if you're using the pesto for a pizza, be careful not to salt it too much; as it cooks on the pizza, the flavors will intensify.)

CARAMELIZED ONIONS

MAKES ABOUT 1 CUP

If you let sliced onions cook long enough in a little oil, they'll transform into tender, sweet "worms"—just like the ones the Turtles find squirming around the sewers of NYC. These are used in several of the recipes. Just make sure they don't slither away!

INGREDIENTS

- 1 tablespoon unsalted butter or extra-virgin olive oil
- 1 ½ medium yellow onions, halved and thinly sliced
- Big pinch of fine sea salt

INSTRUCTIONS

1. Melt the butter or heat the oil in a medium, heavy-bottomed skillet or cast-iron pan over medium heat.

2. Throw in the onions and salt and cook for about 25 minutes, stirring intermittently, until the onions are soft and brown . . . just like worms. If the onions look like they are burning and/or the skillet dries out too fast, sprinkle in a little water and continue cooking until the onions are caramelized.

3. Remove the skillet from heat and set it aside to cool. If you don't plan on making pizza right away, store the onions in an airtight container in the refrigerator for up to 1 week or in the freezer for up to 6 months.

ROASTED GARLIC

MAKES 1
HEAD OF GARLIC

When you want garlicky flavor without the spiciness, roasted is the way to go. Make a double batch and keep it in your fridge for spreading on pizza dough, sandwiches, and anything else that would benefit from some mellow, umami goodness.

INGREDIENTS

1 head garlic

1 tablespoon extra-virgin olive oil

INSTRUCTIONS

1. Preheat the oven to 400°F.

2. Cut off the top ¼ inch of the garlic head to expose the cloves. Place the head cut-side up on a square of aluminum foil.

3. Drizzle with the olive oil, then wrap it up tightly in the foil.

4. Roast the garlic for about 45 minutes or until the cloves are very soft.

5. Remove from the oven and carefully open the foil packet.

6. Let the garlic cool for at least 10 minutes, then squeeze the roasted garlic cloves into a small bowl or container. The roasted garlic will keep in an airtight container in the refrigerator for up to 2 weeks.

DID YOU KNOW, BRO?
RUMOR HAS IT THAT SHREDDER'S ARMOR IS MODELED AFTER A COMMON KITCHEN TOOL: THE CHEESE GRATER. TMNT COCREATOR KEVIN EASTMAN CAME ACROSS A LARGE, TRIANGULAR GRATER WHILE DOING THE DISHES AT HOME AND THOUGHT IT WOULD MAKE THE IDEAL WEAPON FOR A NINJA VILLAIN.

OLD SCHOOL

SOMETIMES THE TURTLES ARE TOTALLY DOWN TO SNEAK THROUGH THE SHADOWS DISGUISED IN TRENCH COATS JUST TO GET TO ROY'S PIZZA. OTHER TIMES, IT'S WAY TOO MUCH OF A HASSLE—PLUS, THEY NEVER KNOW WHEN SHREDDER MIGHT BE SETTING UP ANOTHER ONE OF HIS NASTY TRAPS! THAT'S WHY THEY LEARNED TO MAKE ALL THE STANDARD PIZZERIA MENU ITEMS DOWN IN THE LAIR. HERE ARE SOME OF THE MOST CLASSIC OLD SCHOOL PIZZERIA ORDERS:

NEW YORK-STYLE PEPPERONI PIZZA

MAKES ONE 12-INCH PIZZA

Raph's a purist when it comes to pizza, and this one is just how he likes it—straight to the point, covered with pepperoni, and finished with a ka-pow of spicy red pepper flakes. If you need to tone it down, just skip the flakes and serve it pizza shop-style with shakers of dried oregano, garlic salt, and Parmesan on the side.

INGREDIENTS

Cornmeal or flour for dusting

Extra-virgin olive oil for brushing and greasing

1-pound ball pizza dough, homemade (pages 17-19) or store-bought

½ to ⅔ cup New York-Style Pizza Sauce (page 23)

¾ cup shredded low-moisture mozzarella cheese

4 tablespoons freshly grated Parmesan cheese

3 ounces sliced pepperoni

Pinch of crushed red pepper flakes (optional)

INSTRUCTIONS

BAKING STONE:
Place your baking stone on the middle rack of the oven and preheat to 500°F for at least 30 minutes, then turn the oven to broil. Dust a pizza peel or inverted baking sheet with cornmeal or flour.

BAKING SHEET:
Preheat the oven to 500°F with a rack in the middle position. Lightly coat a heavy-duty, rimmed baking sheet with olive oil.

1. Stretch or roll the dough into a 12-inch disk and place it on the prepared pizza peel or baking sheet.

2. Spread the sauce on the dough, leaving a 1-inch border all around. Sprinkle on the mozzarella, then 2 tablespoons of the Parmesan, and arrange the pepperoni slices on top.

3. Finish with the remaining 2 tablespoons of Parmesan. Brush the exposed dough with olive oil.

4. Shimmy the dough from the peel to the hot baking stone or transfer the baking sheet to the oven.

5. Bake until the crust is golden, the cheese is melted, and the toppings are just beginning to blister (6 to 8 minutes on the baking stone; 10 to 15 minutes on the baking sheet).

6. Remove the pizza from the oven and let it cool for 5 minutes, then sprinkle with red pepper flakes, if using. Slice and serve.

Lighten It Up, DUDE!

USE WHOLE-WHEAT PIZZA DOUGH (PAGE 18) AND LOW-FAT MOZZARELLA.

OLD-SCHOOL ITALIAN

MAKES ONE
12-INCH PIZZA

When Princess Mallory visited the lair, the Turtles served this pie, hoping she would be impressed by their super-refined, sophisticated taste.

INGREDIENTS

Cornmeal or flour for dusting

Extra-virgin olive oil for drizzling and greasing

1-pound ball pizza dough, homemade (pages 17-19) or store-bought

1/2 to 2/3 cup No-Cook Tomato Sauce (page 21)

3 to 4 ounces fresh mozzarella cheese, cut into 1/4-inch-thick slices

4 or 5 fresh basil leaves, torn

Pinch of fine sea salt

INSTRUCTIONS

BAKING STONE/STEEL:
Place your baking stone on the middle rack of the oven and preheat to 500°F for at least 30 minutes, then turn the oven to broil. Dust a pizza peel or inverted baking sheet with cornmeal or flour.

BAKING SHEET:
Preheat the oven to 500°F with a rack in the middle position. Lightly coat a heavy-duty, rimmed baking sheet with olive oil.

1. Stretch or roll the dough into a 12-inch disk and place it on the prepared pizza peel or baking sheet.

2. Spread the sauce on the dough, leaving a 1-inch border all around, then arrange the mozzarella slices on top. Brush the exposed dough with olive oil.

3. Shimmy the dough from the peel to the hot baking stone or transfer the baking sheet to the oven

4. Bake until the crust is golden, the cheese is melted, and the toppings are just beginning to blister (6 to 8 minutes on the baking stone; 10 to 15 minutes on the baking sheet).

5. Remove the pizza from the oven and let it cool for 5 minutes, then scatter the torn basil leaves over the top, sprinkle with sea salt, and finish with a light drizzle of olive oil. Slice and serve.

DID YOU KNOW, BRO?
PIZZA MARGHERITA—WITH TOMATOES, MOZZARELLA, AND BASIL—WAS NAMED AFTER QUEEN MARGHERITA OF ITALY IN 1889 AFTER SHE DECLARED IT HER FAVORITE COMBINATION OF TOPPINGS DURING A VISIT TO NAPLES.

Lighten It Up, DUDE!

USE WHOLE-WHEAT PIZZA DOUGH (PAGE 18) AND LOW-FAT CHEESE.

MIKEY'S MEATZZA MAYHEM

MAKES ONE 12-INCH PIZZA

Can't decide which meat topping to put on your pizza? Do what Michelangelo does—use all of them! This version is topped with sausage, ground beef, bacon, and pepperoni, but you can mix and match with any cured and cooked meats you like.

INGREDIENTS

Cornmeal or flour for dusting

2 teaspoons extra-virgin olive oil, divided, plus more for brushing and greasing

1/4 pound sweet or hot Italian sausage, casing removed

1/4 pound ground beef

2 slices thick-cut bacon, chopped

1-pound ball pizza dough, homemade (pages 17-19) or store-bought

1/2 to 2/3 cup New York-Style Pizza Sauce (page 23)

1 large garlic clove, very thinly sliced

3/4 cup shredded low-moisture mozzarella cheese

8 slices pepperoni

Pinch of crushed red pepper flakes (optional)

INSTRUCTIONS

BAKING STONE/STEEL:
Place your baking stone on the middle rack of the oven and preheat to 500°F for at least 30 minutes, then turn the oven to broil. Dust a pizza peel or inverted baking sheet with cornmeal or flour.

BAKING SHEET:
Preheat the oven to 500°F with a rack in the middle position. Lightly coat a heavy-duty, rimmed baking sheet with olive oil.

1. Heat 1 teaspoon of the olive oil in a medium skillet over medium heat. Crumble in the sausage and cook for 3 to 5 minutes or until browned, breaking it up with a wooden spoon. Transfer the sausage to a paper towel–lined plate.

2. Wipe out the skillet and place it back over medium heat. Repeat step 1 with the ground beef.

3. Wipe out the skillet one more time and place it back over medium heat. Add the bacon and cook for about 5 minutes or until the fat has rendered and the bacon just begins to crisp at the edges. Remove the pan from the heat and transfer the bacon to a paper towel–lined plate.

4. Stretch or roll the dough into a 12-inch disk and place it on the prepared pizza peel or baking sheet.

5. Spread the sauce on the dough, leaving a 1/2-inch border all around. Arrange the garlic slices on top of the sauce, followed by half of the cheese, then the meats, and finally the remaining cheese. Brush the exposed dough with olive oil. Shimmy the dough from the peel to the hot baking stone or transfer the baking sheet to the oven.

6. Bake until the crust is golden and the cheese just begins to brown in spots (6 to 8 minutes on the baking stone; 10 to 15 minutes on the baking sheet).

7. Remove the pizza from the oven and let it cool for 5 minutes, then sprinkle with red pepper flakes, if using. Slice and serve.

DID YOU KNOW, BRO?
PINEAPPLE AND HAM PIZZA—BETTER KNOWN AS HAWAIIAN—MAY SEEM LIKE A TROPICAL INVENTION, BUT AS MASTER SPLINTER WOULD SAY, "ALL IS NOT WHAT IT SEEMS." THIS CLASSIC TOPPING COMBINATION WAS ACTUALLY CREATED BY A RESTAURANT OWNER IN ONTARIO, CANADA, IN 1962.

THE SEWER SURFER

MAKES ONE
12-INCH PIZZA

After catching a ride on the algae-green waves of the sewer, the brothers crave this radical pie topped with red sauce, chunks of ham and juicy pineapple, and lots of oozy mozzarella.

INGREDIENTS

Cornmeal or flour for dusting

Extra-virgin olive oil for brushing and greasing

1-pound ball pizza dough, homemade (pages 17-19) or store-bought

$1/2$ to $2/3$ cup New York-Style Pizza Sauce (page 23)

$3/4$ cup grated low-moisture mozzarella cheese

1 cup diced ham, cooked

1 cup diced fresh pineapple

INSTRUCTIONS

BAKING STONE/STEEL:
Place your baking stone on the middle rack of the oven and preheat to 500°F for at least 30 minutes, then turn the oven to broil. Dust a pizza peel or inverted baking sheet with cornmeal or flour.

BAKING SHEET:
Preheat the oven to 500°F with a rack in the middle position. Lightly coat a heavy-duty, rimmed baking sheet with olive oil.

1. Stretch or roll the dough into a 12-inch disk and place it on the prepared pizza peel or baking sheet.

2. Spread the sauce on the dough, leaving a 1-inch border all around. Sprinkle on the mozzarella, then the ham and pineapple. Brush the exposed dough with olive oil.

3. Shimmy the dough from the peel to the hot baking stone or transfer the baking sheet to the oven.

4. Bake until the crust is golden, the cheese is melted, and the toppings are just beginning to blister (6 to 8 minutes on the baking stone; 10 to 15 minutes on the baking sheet).

5. Remove the pizza from the oven and let it cool for 5 minutes before slicing.

Lighten It Up, DUDE!

USE WHOLE-WHEAT PIZZA DOUGH (PAGE 18) AND LOW-FAT MOZZARELLA.

SAUSAGE AND PEPPER POW!

MAKES ONE 12-INCH PIZZA

You might need a knife and fork for this one—and plenty of napkins. This classic Italian-American flavor combo can be found in sandwich and pizza shops throughout New York City. This pizza can also be a crowd-pleaser at any Turtle-riffic party!

INGREDIENTS

Cornmeal or flour for dusting

2 teaspoons extra-virgin olive oil, divided, plus more for brushing and greasing

½ pound sweet or hot Italian sausage, casings removed

½ large green bell pepper, seeded and sliced

½ medium yellow onion, halved and sliced

1-pound ball pizza dough, homemade (pages 17-19) or store-bought

⅓ cup No-Cook Tomato Sauce (page 21)

¾ cup shredded low-moisture mozzarella

Lighten It Up, DUDE!

USE WHOLE-WHEAT PIZZA DOUGH (PAGE 18), VEGAN OR TURKEY SAUSAGE, AND LOW-FAT MOZZARELLA.

INSTRUCTIONS

BAKING STONE/STEEL:
Place your baking stone on the middle rack of the oven and preheat to 500°F for at least 30 minutes, then turn the oven to broil. Dust a pizza peel or inverted baking sheet with cornmeal or flour.

BAKING SHEET:
Preheat the oven to 500°F with a rack in the middle position. Lightly coat a heavy-duty, rimmed baking sheet with olive oil.

1. Put 1 teaspoon of the oil in a medium heavy-bottomed skillet or cast-iron pan and set it over medium heat. When the oil starts to ripple, crumble in the sausage and cook it for about 3 minutes, breaking it up with a wooden spoon until it's no longer pink. Remove the sausage from the skillet using a slotted spoon and place it on a paper towel–lined plate to drain.

2. Add the remaining teaspoon of oil to the skillet, still over medium heat, and throw in the pepper and onion. Cook, stirring every minute or two, until the vegetables are soft and beginning to brown, about 5 minutes.

3. When the pepper and onion are done cooking, turn off the heat. Return the sausage to the pan and toss well. Set aside to cool.

4. Stretch or roll the dough into a 12-inch disk and place it on the prepared pizza peel or baking sheet.

5. Spoon the tomato sauce onto the dough and spread it out evenly, leaving a ½-inch border of dough all around.

6. Scatter on the cheese, and then arrange the sausage, pepper, and onion mixture on top.

7. Shimmy the dough from the peel to the hot baking stone or transfer the baking sheet to the oven.

8. Bake until the crust is golden and the cheese is just beginning to brown in spots (6 to 8 minutes on the baking stone; 10 to 15 minutes on the baking sheet).

9. Remove the pizza from the oven and let it cool for 5 minutes, then slice and serve.

SNOWMAGEDDON

MAKES ONE 12-INCH PIZZA

Creamy white sauce and ricotta make this "white pizza" an ooey gooey favorite at pizza shops all over the country.

INGREDIENTS

Cornmeal or flour for dusting

Extra-virgin olive oil for brushing, drizzling, and greasing

1 cup ricotta cheese

1 teaspoon chopped fresh oregano (or ½ teaspoon dried)

Salt and freshly ground black pepper

1-pound ball pizza dough, homemade (pages 17-19) or store-bought

½ to ⅔ cup White Pizza Sauce (page 24)

Lighten It Up, DUDE! USE WHOLE-WHEAT PIZZA DOUGH (PAGE 18) AND LOW-FAT RICOTTA.

INSTRUCTIONS

BAKING STONE/STEEL:
Place your baking stone on the middle rack of the oven and preheat to 500°F for at least 30 minutes, then turn the oven to broil. Dust a pizza peel or inverted baking sheet with cornmeal or flour.

BAKING SHEET:
Preheat the oven to 500°F with a rack in the middle position. Lightly coat a heavy-duty, rimmed baking sheet with olive oil.

1. In a small bowl, mix together the ricotta and oregano. Season to taste with salt and pepper.

2. Stretch or roll the dough into a 12-inch disk and place it on the prepared pizza peel or baking sheet.

3. Spread the pizza sauce on the dough, leaving a ½-inch border all around. Spoon dollops of the ricotta mixture all over the pizza. Brush the exposed dough with olive oil.

4. Shimmy the dough from the peel to the hot baking stone or transfer the baking sheet to the oven.

5. Bake until the crust is golden and the cheese is just beginning to brown in spots (6 to 8 minutes on the baking stone; 10 to 15 minutes on the baking sheet).

6. Remove the pizza from the oven and let it cool for 5 minutes. Finish with a light drizzle of olive oil, a pinch of salt, and a grind or two of black pepper. Slice and serve.

RAPH'S RUDE 'SHROOMS

MAKES ONE
12-INCH PIZZA

The flavor of this pie is cool but rude, just like Raphael! It's piled with garlic, mushrooms, onions, and fontina cheese, so prepare yourself for some serious ninja breath. You might not think it's rude, but the next person who talks to you will!

INGREDIENTS

Cornmeal or flour for dusting

1 tablespoon extra-virgin olive oil, plus more for brushing and greasing

8 ounces cremini mushrooms, sliced

1 large garlic clove, pressed or minced

1-pound ball pizza dough, homemade (pages 17-19) or store-bought

1/2 to 2/3 cup New York-Style Pizza Sauce (page 23)

1/2 cup shredded low-moisture mozzarella

1/2 cup shredded fontina or Gruyère cheese

3/4 to 1 cup caramelized onions (page 28)

1 tablespoon chopped fresh rosemary

Lighten It Up, DUDE!
USE WHOLE-WHEAT PIZZA DOUGH (PAGE 18) AND LOW-FAT RICOTTA.

INSTRUCTIONS

BAKING STONE/STEEL:
Place your baking stone on the middle rack of the oven and preheat to 500°F for at least 30 minutes, then turn the oven to broil. Dust a pizza peel or inverted baking sheet with cornmeal or flour.

BAKING SHEET:
Preheat the oven to 500°F with a rack in the middle position. Lightly coat a heavy-duty, rimmed baking sheet with olive oil.

1. Warm the oil in a medium skillet over medium heat. Add the mushrooms and cook for 5 minutes, stirring frequently, until they are tender and most of the liquid has evaporated. Toss in the garlic, stir well, and remove the skillet from the heat.

2. Stretch or roll the dough into a 12-inch disk and place it on the prepared pizza peel or baking sheet.

3. Spoon the tomato sauce onto the dough and spread it out evenly, leaving a ½-inch border of dough all around. Scatter on the cheeses, then arrange the mushrooms and caramelized onions on top.

4. Shimmy the dough from the peel to the hot baking stone or transfer the baking sheet to the oven.

5. Bake until the crust is golden and the cheese is just beginning to brown in spots (6 to 8 minutes on the baking stone; 10 to 15 minutes on the baking sheet).

6. Remove the pizza from the oven and let it rest for 5 minutes. Sprinkle on the rosemary and then slice and serve.

FOUR-CHEESE FOR FOUR BROS

MAKES ONE 12-INCH PIZZA

Once, to snap the Turtles out of a bummer mood, Master Splinter brought them a pizza topped with ninety-nine different cheeses. Of course it did the trick. This isn't that gnarly, but it's a start!

INGREDIENTS

Cornmeal or flour for dusting

2 tablespoons extra-virgin olive oil, plus more for drizzling and greasing

1 large garlic clove, pressed or grated

1-pound ball pizza dough, homemade (pages 17-19) or store-bought

Fine sea salt and freshly ground black pepper

½ cup shredded low-moisture mozzarella

¼ cup shredded Monterey Jack cheese

½ cup ricotta cheese

3 tablespoons grated Parmesan cheese

1 tablespoon chopped fresh parsley leaves

Lighten It Up, DUDE!

USE WHOLE-WHEAT PIZZA DOUGH (PAGE 18) AND LOW-FAT MOZZARELLA AND RICOTTA.

INSTRUCTIONS

BAKING STONE/STEEL:
Place your baking stone on the middle rack of the oven and preheat to 500°F for at least 30 minutes. Dust a pizza peel or inverted baking sheet with cornmeal or flour.

BAKING SHEET:
Preheat the oven to 500°F with a rack in the middle position. Lightly coat a heavy-duty, rimmed baking sheet with olive oil.

1. In a small bowl, stir together the olive oil and garlic. Set aside to marinate for 15 minutes.

2. Stretch or roll the dough into a 12-inch disk and place it on the prepared pizza peel or baking sheet.

3. Brush the dough all over with some of the garlic oil, making sure to get it all the way to the edges.

4. Season with salt and pepper, scatter on the mozzarella and Jack cheeses, dot all over with ricotta, and sprinkle the Parmesan over the top.

5. Shimmy the dough from the peel to the hot baking stone or transfer the baking sheet to the oven.

6. Bake the pizza for 8 to 15 minutes until the crust is golden brown and the cheese is beginning to blister in spots.

7. Remove the pizza from the oven, season with a light drizzle of olive oil, and sprinkle with the parsley. Let it chill at room temperature for 5 minutes, then slice and serve.

VEGGIE VICTORY

MAKES ONE 12-INCH PIZZA

Veggies bring vigor. Veggies bring vitality. Veggies bring muscles. So veggies bring victory! Paired with mozzarella and creamy pesto, this pizza is just what the Turtles need to keep in crime-fighting shape.

INGREDIENTS

Cornmeal or flour for dusting

1 tablespoon extra-virgin olive oil, plus more for greasing

½ small eggplant, sliced

½ medium red bell pepper, seeded and sliced

½ medium zucchini, sliced

Salt and freshly ground black pepper

1 pound ball pizza dough, homemade (pages 17-19) or store-bought

⅓ to ½ cup pesto, homemade (page 27) or store-bought

¾ cup shredded low-moisture mozzarella

Lighten It Up, DUDE!

SWAP THE PESTO WITH NO-COOK TOMATO SAUCE (PAGE 21). USE WHOLE-WHEAT PIZZA DOUGH (PAGE 18) AND LOW-FAT MOZZARELLA.

INSTRUCTIONS

BAKING STONE/STEEL:
Place your baking stone on the middle rack of the oven and preheat to 400°F. Dust a pizza peel or inverted baking sheet with cornmeal or flour.

BAKING SHEET:
Preheat the oven to 400°F with a rack in the middle position. Line a heavy-duty, rimmed baking sheet with parchment or aluminum foil.

1. Arrange the sliced vegetables on the prepared baking sheet and drizzle them with the oil. Turn to coat. Season with salt and pepper.

2. Roast the vegetables for 15 to 20 minutes or until they are tender and browned. Remove them from the oven and set aside to cool.

3. Increase the oven temperature to 500°F and let it heat up for at least 20 minutes. If you're using the same baking sheet to bake your pizza, transfer the roasted veggies to a plate.

4. Remove the parchment or foil and rub the baking sheet lightly with olive oil. If you're using a pizza stone or steel, turn the oven to broil.

5. Stretch or roll the dough into a 12-inch disk and place it on the prepared pizza peel or baking sheet.

6. Scoop the pesto onto the dough and spread it out evenly, leaving a ½-inch border of dough all around. Scatter on half of the cheese, then the roasted vegetables, and finish with the rest of the cheese.

7. Shimmy the dough from the peel to the hot baking stone or transfer the baking sheet to the oven.

8. Bake until the crust is golden and the cheese is just beginning to brown in spots (6 to 8 minutes on the baking stone; 10 to 15 minutes on the baking sheet).

9. Remove the pizza from the oven and let it rest for 5 minutes, then slice and serve.

NEW SCHOOL

CALLING ALL PARTY DUDES! IF YOU'D PICK MAC ATTACK (PAGE 55) OVER PLAIN PIZZA ANY DAY, THEN THIS IS THE CHAPTER FOR YOU. STRETCH YOUR PIZZA IMAGINATION TO THE MAX WITH:

- DEEP-DISH GOULASH PIZZA (PAGE 49)
- CHOCOLATE-CHILI PEPPER PIZZA WITH BUTTERNUT SQUASH (PAGE 50)
- BBQ CHICKEN PIZZA (PAGE 52)
- PERSONAL PORTOBELLO PIZZAS (PAGE 53)
- THE MAC ATTACK (PAGE 55)
- THE BREAKFAST PIE (PAGE 57)
- PIZZA PORTRAITS (PAGE 58)
- SLUDGE PIE (PAGE 60)
- OMELET IN A HALF SHELL (PAGE 61)
- HOLY GUACAMOLE! (PAGE 63)
- SHAKSHUKA PIZZA (PAGE 64)

- THE BLT (PAGE 65)
- MIGHTY MEATBALL AND SAUERKRAUT PIZZA (PAGE 66)
- LEO'S KATANA SLASHES (PAGE 69)
- MU SHU PORK PIE (PAGE 70)
- ANCHOVY PIZZA WITH EXTRA GARLIC (PAGE 71)
- THE APRIL O' NEIL (PAGE 73)
- SHREDDER'S REVENGE (PAGE 74)
- THE LEAN, MEAN, AND GREEN (PAGE 75)
- TOTAL TUNA MELTDOWN (PAGE 77)
- PEPPERONI AND SWEET PICKLE PIE (PAGE 79)
- CRAZY CORN AND BODACIOUS BEAN PIZZA (PAGE 81)

BUT DON'T WORRY—THOUGH THEY MAY BE BASED ON MIKEY'S CRAZY PIZZA ORDERS, ALL THE RECIPES THAT FOLLOW ARE CREATED FOR HUMAN APPETITES.

DEEP-DISH GOULASH PIZZA

MAKES ONE
DEEP-DISH PIZZA

When the Turtles need to power up, they grab a slice of this hearty pie. Crammed full of macaroni, ground beef, vegetables, and mozzarella, it's perfect after a serious showdown with Shredder.

INGREDIENTS

2 cups elbow macaroni

1 tablespoon extra-virgin olive oil, plus more for greasing

1-pound ball One-Hour Dough (page 19) or store-bought pizza dough

1/2 pound lean ground beef

1 tablespoon paprika

1/2 large yellow onion, chopped

1/2 large red bell pepper, seeded and chopped

1 garlic clove, minced or pressed

One 15-ounce can tomato sauce

One 15-ounce can diced tomatoes, drained

1/2 teaspoon salt

1/4 teaspoon freshly ground black pepper

3/4 cup shredded Monterey Jack cheese

1 tablespoon chopped fresh parsley

INSTRUCTIONS

1. Bring a large pot of water to a boil and cook the macaroni to al dente. Drain well.

2. Rub the inside of a cast-iron skillet, deep-dish pie plate, or spring-form pan with olive oil.

3. Drop the dough into the pan and, using your fingers, press it out along the bottom and 2 inches up the sides. Cover with a damp kitchen towel and set aside to rest while you make the goulash.

4. Preheat the oven to 450°F.

5. Heat the oil in a large skillet or saucepan over medium heat. Add the ground beef and cook, breaking it up with a wooden spoon, for 3 to 5 minutes or until it's no longer pink.

6. Add the paprika, onion, bell pepper, and garlic and cook, stirring frequently, until the vegetables are tender (6 to 8 minutes).

7. Dump in the tomato sauce and diced tomatoes and season with the salt and pepper. Cook for 15 to 20 minutes or until the sauce has thickened.

8. Taste and add more salt and pepper if needed, then stir in the cooked macaroni. Remove the skillet from the heat.

9. Uncover the dough. Sprinkle on half of the cheese, then add enough goulash to fill the pan. (Transfer any leftovers to an airtight container and store it in the fridge for up to 1 week or in the freezer for up to 2 months.)

10. Finish with the remaining cheese and bake the pizza for 25 minutes or until the crust is golden and the cheese is bubbly and just starting to brown in spots.

11. Remove the pizza from the oven. Let it rest for at least 5 minutes, then sprinkle with parsley. Slice and serve.

Lighten It Up, DUDE!

USE WHOLE-WHEAT MACARONI; GROUND TURKEY, CHICKEN, OR CRUMBLED EXTRA-FIRM TOFU INSTEAD OF THE GROUND BEEF; AND WHOLE-WHEAT PIZZA DOUGH (PAGE 18).

CHOCOLATE-CHILI PEPPER PIZZA WITH BUTTERNUT SQUASH

MAKES ONE 12-INCH PIZZA

Michelangelo's a big fan of chocolate fudge on pizza. Mole is a traditional savory chocolate sauce from Mexico. Add the spiciness of chili pepper and the richness of butternut squash, and you get a new and surprising hit. It's a no-brainer, bro.

INGREDIENTS

2 cups cubed butternut squash (½-inch pieces)

1 teaspoon plus 2 tablespoons olive oil, plus more for greasing

Fine sea salt and freshly ground black pepper

1 large yellow onion, chopped

3 medium garlic cloves, pressed or minced

1 or 2 chipotle chilies in adobo sauce, chopped

2 teaspoons chili powder

1 teaspoon ground cumin

2 tablespoons smooth natural peanut butter

Handful of corn tortilla chips

1 teaspoon dried oregano

1 ¾ cups low-sodium chicken broth

3 ounces unsweetened dark chocolate, chopped

Cornmeal or flour for dusting

1-pound ball pizza dough, homemade (pages 17-19) or store-bought

¾ cup shredded Jack cheese

1 to 2 tablespoons finely sliced scallions (white and light green parts only)

¼ cup sour cream

2 tablespoons crumbled queso fresco or mild feta cheese

INSTRUCTIONS

TO MAKE THE SQUASH

1. Preheat the oven to 400°F with racks in the center and bottom third positions. (If you're using a baking stone/steel, place it on the bottom rack.)

2. Dump the cubed squash onto a heavy-duty, rimmed baking sheet; toss it with 1 teaspoon of the oil; and season lightly with salt and pepper (about ⅛ teaspoon of each).

3. Roast for about 30 minutes, stirring halfway through, until the squash is tender and beginning to brown. Remove the squash from the oven and set it aside to cool slightly. Increase the oven temperature to 500°F.

TO MAKE THE MOLE

1. While the squash roasts, make the chocolate (aka mole) sauce. Heat the remaining 2 tablespoons of oil in a large skillet or saucepan over medium-high heat. Add the onion to the pan, give it a pinch of salt, and cook, stirring frequently, until the onions begin to soften up a bit (3 to 5 minutes). Toss in the garlic and cook for one more minute, stirring constantly.

2. Transfer the onion and garlic mixture to a blender or food processor, along with the chipotle(s), chili powder, cumin, peanut butter, tortilla chips, oregano, and chicken broth. Puree until the mixture is smooth and uniform in color.

3. Pour this mixture into a medium saucepan and place it over high heat. When it begins to boil, reduce the heat to medium, cover the pan, and cook for 20 to 25 minutes to let the flavors marry and intensify.

4. Remove the lid and stir in the chocolate until it is completely melted. Taste the sauce and add more salt and pepper if desired.

5. Remove the pan from the heat and set it aside to cool slightly.

USE WHOLE-WHEAT PIZZA DOUGH (PAGE 18). USE SALT-FREE CHILI POWDER, MAKE SURE YOUR NATURAL PEANUT BUTTER CONTAINS ONLY PEANUTS—NO EXTRA SALT OR OTHER ADDITIVES—AND SWAP THE SOUR CREAM WITH PLAIN, LOW-FAT YOGURT.

FOR ASSEMBLY

BAKING STONE/STEEL:
Dust a pizza peel or inverted baking sheet with cornmeal or flour.

BAKING SHEET:
Lightly coat a heavy-duty, rimmed baking sheet with olive oil.

1. Stretch or roll the dough into a 12-inch disk and place it on the prepared pizza peel or baking sheet.

2. In a medium bowl, toss the roasted squash with ⅓ cup of the mole sauce.

3. Spoon about ⅓ cup of the remaining mole sauce onto the dough and spread it out evenly, leaving a ¼-inch border of dough all around.*

4. Transfer the mole-coated squash to the dough and arrange it in a single layer. Top with the Jack cheese.

5. Shimmy the pizza from the peel to the hot baking stone or transfer the baking sheet to the oven.

6. Bake for 8 to 15 minutes or until the crust is golden brown.

7. Remove the pizza from the oven and let it rest for 5 minutes. Sprinkle on the scallions.

8. Scoop the sour cream into a small, resealable plastic bag and snip off the tip of one of the bottom corners.

9. Pipe the sour cream in a zigzag pattern over the pizza and sprinkle on the queso fresco. Slice and serve.

*Save the remaining mole sauce for dipping pizza crust or tortilla chips. It will keep in an airtight container in the fridge for up to 1 week.

BBQ CHICKEN PIZZA

MAKES ONE
12-INCH PIZZA

In the summer, when the aroma of fire-escape cookouts wafts down through the sewer grate, the Turtles get a hankering for pies like this one. Slathered with barbecue sauce and topped with cheddar cheese, the BBQ chicken pizza is a modern classic. Who needs a backyard anyway?

INGREDIENTS

Cornmeal or flour for dusting

Extra-virgin olive oil for greasing

1 cooked chicken breast, thinly sliced

2/3 cup barbecue sauce, divided

1-pound ball pizza dough, homemade (pages 17-19) or store-bought

3/4 cup shredded low-moisture mozzarella

1/4 cup shredded sharp cheddar cheese

1/4 cup sliced scallions

Lighten It Up, DUDE!

POACH THE CHICKEN BREAST, USE AN ALL-NATURAL BARBECUE SAUCE, AND OPT FOR LOW-FAT MOZZARELLA AND WHOLE-WHEAT PIZZA DOUGH (PAGE 18).

INSTRUCTIONS

BAKING STONE/STEEL:
Place baking stone on the middle rack of the oven and preheat to 500°F for at least 30 minutes, then turn the oven to broil. Dust a pizza peel or inverted baking sheet with cornmeal or flour.

BAKING SHEET:
Preheat the oven to 500°F with a rack in the middle position. Lightly coat a heavy-duty, rimmed baking sheet with olive oil.

1. In a medium bowl, toss the chicken with 1/3 cup of the barbecue sauce.

2. Stretch or roll the dough into a 12-inch disk and place it on the prepared pizza peel or baking sheet.

3. Spread the remaining 1/3 cup of barbecue sauce on the dough, leaving a 1/2-inch border of dough all around.

4. Arrange the chicken on top in an even layer, then top with the mozzarella and cheddar cheeses.

5. Shimmy the dough from the peel to the hot baking stone or transfer the baking sheet to the oven.

6. Bake until the crust is golden and the cheese is just beginning to brown in spots (6 to 8 minutes on the baking stone; 10 to 15 minutes on the baking sheet).

7. Remove the pizza from the oven. Let it rest for 5 minutes, then sprinkle with the scallions. Slice and serve.

PERSONAL PORTOBELLO PIZZAS

MAKES 4
PERSONAL PIZZAS

When there are four brothers, sharing can be a little bit of a, uh, challenge. These sturdy portobello mushrooms can handle all sorts of different toppings, and the personal portions stop all arguments about sharing before they even start!

INGREDIENTS

4 extra-large portobello mushroom caps, stems, and ribs removed

1 cup No-Cook Tomato Sauce (page 21)

¼ cup shredded low-moisture mozzarella

12 slices pepperoni

2 tablespoons grated Parmesan cheese

1 tablespoon chopped fresh basil

INSTRUCTIONS

1. Preheat the oven to 400°F. Line a heavy-duty, rimmed baking sheet with parchment or aluminum foil.

2. Place the mushrooms on the prepared baking sheet, rib-side up.

3. Fill each one with ¼ cup pizza sauce, then top each with 1 tablespoon mozzarella and three slices of pepperoni.

4. Sprinkle each mushroom with ½ tablespoon of Parmesan.

5. Bake the mushrooms for 20 to 25 minutes until they're bubbly and golden brown.

6. Remove them from the oven and let cool for at least 5 minutes. Sprinkle with the basil and serve.

Lighten It Up, DUDE!

USE LOW-FAT MOZZARELLA AND SKIP THE PEPPERONI.

USE WHOLE-WHEAT MACARONI, WHOLE-WHEAT PIZZA DOUGH (PAGE 18), 1-PERCENT MILK, LOW-FAT CHEESE, AND HALF-AND-HALF INSTEAD OF HEAVY CREAM.

Lighten It Up, **DUDE!**

THE MAC ATTACK

MAKES ONE 12-INCH PIZZA

Can't decide whether you want mac and cheese or pizza? On this mega-awesome pizza, you can have them both at the same time!

INGREDIENTS

Cornmeal or flour for dusting

Extra-virgin olive oil for brushing and greasing

2 cups uncooked elbow macaroni

1 ½ cups whole or low-fat milk

2 tablespoons unsalted butter

2 tablespoons all-purpose flour

Salt and freshly ground black pepper

¼ teaspoon paprika

½ teaspoon Dijon mustard

1 cup shredded white cheddar cheese, divided

1 cup shredded Gruyère cheese, divided

1 heaping tablespoon minced fresh chives, plus more for garnish

½ cup heavy cream

1-pound ball pizza dough, homemade (pages 17-19) or store-bought

INSTRUCTIONS

BAKING STONE/STEEL: Place your baking stone on the middle rack of the oven and preheat to 500°F. Dust a pizza peel or inverted baking sheet with cornmeal or flour.

BAKING SHEET: Preheat the oven to 500°F with a rack in the middle position. Lightly coat a heavy-duty, rimmed baking sheet with olive oil.

1. Bring a pot of salted water to a boil and cook the pasta to al dente, according to the package directions. Drain well.

2. Pour the milk into a small saucepan and warm it over medium-low heat just until it starts to steam; don't let it boil.

3. In a separate, heavy-bottomed saucepan, melt the butter over medium-high heat. Whisk in the flour and cook, whisking constantly, until it forms a smooth, bubbly paste. (Be careful not to let it brown). Whisk in the hot milk for 3 to 5 minutes or until the sauce thickens. Season to taste with salt and pepper. Bring the sauce to a boil, reduce the heat to low, and cook for 2 minutes.

4. Remove from heat. Stir in the paprika, mustard, ¾ cup of the cheddar, and ¾ cup of the Gruyère. Stir until the cheeses are completely melted, then add the chives, cream, and pasta. Mix gently until well combined, then taste and season with additional salt and pepper as desired.

5. Stretch or roll the dough into a 12-inch disk and place it on the prepared pizza peel or baking sheet. Brush the dough with olive oil, then shimmy it from the peel to the hot baking stone or transfer the baking sheet to the oven. Bake for 5 minutes or just until the edges of the crust begin to brown.

6. Remove the crust from the oven. Spread the mac and cheese onto the crust, leaving a ½-inch border of dough all around. Use just enough mac and cheese to make a ¼-inch-thick layer. (Store the leftovers in the refrigerator for up to 1 week.)

7. Sprinkle the remaining ¼ cup of cheddar and ¼ cup of Gruyère over top.

8. Bake the pizza for 8 to 10 minutes or until the crust is blistered and the cheese begins to brown.

9. Remove the pizza from the oven. Let it rest for 5 minutes, then sprinkle with the remaining chopped chives. Slice and serve.

THE BREAKFAST PIE

MAKES ONE 12-INCH PIZZA

The ultimate breakfast . . . or lunch . . . or dinner . . . of champions. Michelangelo likes to top this one off with a splash of hot sauce or a few squirts of ketchup.

INGREDIENTS

Extra-virgin olive oil for greasing

4 slices thick-cut bacon, chopped

1-pound ball pizza dough, homemade (pages 17–19) or store-bought

4 large eggs

³/₄ cup shredded sharp cheddar cheese

¹/₄ cup heavy cream

Fine sea salt and freshly ground black pepper

1 tablespoon finely chopped fresh chives

INSTRUCTIONS

1. Preheat the oven to 500°F with a rack in the middle position. Lightly coat a heavy-duty, rimmed baking sheet with olive oil.

2. Place the bacon in a medium skillet over medium heat and cook until it just begins to crisp (5 to 7 minutes). Remove the skillet from the heat and transfer the bacon to a paper towel–lined plate.

3. Stretch or roll the dough into a 12-inch disk and place it on the prepared baking sheet.

4. Crack the eggs into separate, small prep bowls or ramekins.

5. Scatter the cheese over the dough, followed by the bacon.

6. Drizzle the cream evenly over top, then carefully slide the eggs onto the pizza an inch or two inside the edge, evenly distributed.

7. Season with salt and pepper.

8. Transfer the baking sheet to the oven and bake until the crust is golden, the egg whites are set, and the yolks are still a little squishy (10 to 15 minutes).

9. Remove the pizza from the oven. Let it rest for 5 minutes, then sprinkle with the chives. Slice and serve.

Lighten It Up, DUDE!

USE WHOLE-WHEAT PIZZA DOUGH (PAGE 18), TURKEY OR VEGAN BACON, LOW-FAT CHEESE, AND HALF-AND-HALF INSTEAD OF HEAVY CREAM.

PIZZA PORTRAITS

MAKES 4 PERSONAL PIZZAS

Celebrate your favorite heroes in a half shell with these picture-perfect pizzas.

INGREDIENTS

1 large outer leaf of red cabbage

1 long, thick strip of eggplant skin (at least 6 inches long and 3 inches wide)

Extra-virgin olive oil for brushing and greasing

1 red bell pepper

1 orange bell pepper

1-pound ball One-Hour Dough (page 19) or store-bought pizza dough

1 cup green pesto, homemade (page 27) or store-bought

1 cup black olive tapenade, homemade (page 25) or store-bought

2 whole sundried tomatoes packed in oil

4 mini fresh mozzarella balls (ciliegine)

8 thin slices of black olives

Lighten It Up, DUDE!

USE WHOLE-WHEAT PIZZA DOUGH (PAGE 18) AND LOW-FAT CHEESE.

INSTRUCTIONS

TO MAKE THE MASKS

1. Preheat the oven to 450°F.

2. Bring a medium saucepan of water to a boil.

3. Fill a medium bowl with ice water and place it nearby.

4. Drop the cabbage leaf into the boiling water, pressing it down with a long-handled wooden spoon to make sure it's submerged. Cook for 30 seconds.

5. Immediately transfer the cabbage to the ice water to set its color and stop the cooking. (This will be Leonardo's mask.)

6. Put the eggplant strip in a small baking dish and brush it lightly with oil.

7. Roast for 6 to 8 minutes or until tender, watching to make sure it doesn't burn. (This will be Donatello's mask.)

8. Remove the eggplant from the oven and increase the oven temperature to 500°F.

9. Cut off the tops and bottoms of the bell peppers and make one slit from top to bottom in each tube.

10. Open the peppers, remove the seeds and membranes, and flatten them out, flesh-sides down on a cutting board.

11. Using kitchen shears or a sharp paring knife, cut the peppers into mask shapes.

12. Carefully remove the center rib from the blanched cabbage leaf and then cut a mask shape out of the leaf. Cut the eggplant strip into a mask shape.

13. Set aside the masks.

TO MAKE THE FACES

1. Plop the dough onto a well-floured work surface and cut it into four equally sized pieces. Roll or stretch each piece into a 5- to 6-inch circle.

2. Rub two heavy-duty, rimmed baking sheets with olive oil. Place two circles of dough on each baking sheet and use your fingers to stretch and mold them into the shape of the Turtles' faces.

3. Use your fingers to dimple the dough all over (to prevent bubbling), then brush each dough face with olive oil.

4. Bake for 6 to 8 minutes, rotating the baking sheets halfway through until the crusts are a light golden brown.

5. Remove the baking sheets from the oven and transfer the crusts to a cutting board or serving plate.

6. Spoon the pesto onto the crusts and spread it out evenly all the way to the edges.

7. Press the prepared masks onto the faces.

TO MAKE THE MOUTHS

1. Scoop the tapenade into a resealable plastic bag and snip the tip off of one of the bottom corners.

2. Pipe a mouth of tapenade toward the bottom of each pizza.

3. Using kitchen shears or a sharp paring knife, cut each sundried tomato in half lengthwise and trim each half as needed to make an oblong tongue.

4. Press the tongues into the tapenade mouths.

TO MAKE THE EYES

1. Cut each mini mozzarella ball in half, then cut a thin slice from each half.

2. Place two mozzarella slices on each mask and top each one with an olive-slice pupil.

SLUDGE PIE

MAKES ONE
12-INCH PIZZA

This pizza looks as grimy and gooey as sewer sludge, but, just as with the Turtles, looks can be very deceiving.

INGREDIENTS

Cornmeal or flour for dusting

Extra-virgin olive oil for greasing

1-pound ball pizza dough, homemade (pages 17-19) or store-bought

1 cup green pesto, homemade (page 27) or store-bought

1 cup caramelized onions (page 28)

1/4 cup heavy cream, divided

INSTRUCTIONS

BAKING STONE/STEEL: Place your baking stone on the middle rack of the oven and preheat to 500°F for at least 30 minutes, then turn the oven to broil. Dust a pizza peel or inverted baking sheet with cornmeal or flour.

BAKING SHEET: Preheat the oven to 500°F with a rack in the middle position. Lightly coat a heavy-duty, rimmed baking sheet with olive oil.

1. Stretch or roll the dough into a 12-inch disk and place it on the prepared pizza peel or baking sheet.

2. Scoop the pesto (aka sludge) onto the dough and spread it out evenly, leaving a ½-inch border of dough all around.

3. Scatter on the caramelized onions (aka worms) and drizzle with half of the cream.

4. Shimmy the dough from the peel to the hot baking stone or transfer the baking sheet to the oven.

5. Bake until the crust is golden (6 to 8 minutes on the baking stone; 10 to 15 minutes on the baking sheet).

6. Remove the pizza from the oven and immediately drizzle with the remaining cream. Let rest for 5 minutes, then slice and serve.

DID YOU KNOW, BRO?

IN 2010, BRIAN ELDER BROKE THE GUINNESS WORLD RECORD FOR MOST PIZZAS MADE IN ONE HOUR AT A DOMINO'S PIZZA STORE IN FINDLAY, OHIO. HE ACTUALLY MADE 215, BUT ONLY 206 OF THEM PASSED THE JUDGES' INSPECTIONS.

Lighten It Up, **DUDE!** USE WHOLE-WHEAT PIZZA DOUGH (PAGE 18) AND HALF-AND-HALF INSTEAD OF HEAVY CREAM.

OMELET IN A HALF SHELL

MAKES ONE 12-INCH PIZZA

Pizza—there's no better way to start your day! Feel free to swap out the ham and swiss for your favorite omelet ingredients. But ninja beware—never overcook the eggs in the oven. The dish is done when the eggs are set but still a little wet looking in the middle.

INGREDIENTS

Extra-virgin olive oil for greasing

4 large eggs

1/4 cup whole or low-fat milk

1-pound ball pizza dough, homemade (pages 17-19) or store-bought

3/4 cup shredded Swiss cheese

1 cup diced, cooked ham

Fine sea salt and freshly ground black pepper

INSTRUCTIONS

1. Preheat the oven to 500°F with a rack in the middle position. Lightly coat a heavy-duty, rimmed baking sheet with olive oil.

2. In a medium bowl, whisk together the eggs and milk until fully combined.

3. Stretch or roll the dough into a 12-inch disk and place it on the prepared baking sheet.

4. Scatter the cheese and then the ham over the dough.

5. Slowly pour the egg mixture into the center of the pizza and spread it out carefully, leaving a 1-inch border all around. Season with salt and pepper.

6. Transfer the baking sheet to the oven and bake until the crust is golden and the eggs are set in the middle (8 to 10 minutes).

7. Remove the pizza from the oven. Let it rest for 5 minutes, then slice and serve.

Lighten It Up, **DUDE!**

USE WHOLE-WHEAT PIZZA DOUGH (PAGE 18), LOW-FAT CHEESE, AND LOW-FAT MILK OR WATER TO SCRAMBLE THE EGGS.

DID YOU KNOW, BRO?

THE TURTLE COMMUNICATOR WAS WAY AHEAD OF ITS TIME! IN 2015, MOBILE ORDERING MADE UP 23 PERCENT OF ALL FOOD ORDERS IN THE UNITED STATES.

HOLY GUACAMOLE!

MAKES ONE
12-INCH PIZZA

Avocado, tomato, red onion, and jalapeño are a classic flavor combination. So why not mash them all together on some dough? It's like one giant nacho! If you can't live without the addition of some cheddar cheese, just shred it up and sprinkle it on the crust for the last few minutes of baking.

INGREDIENTS

Cornmeal or flour for dusting

Extra-virgin olive oil for brushing and greasing

1 medium tomato, seeded and finely diced

1 tablespoon chopped fresh cilantro

2 tablespoons minced red onion

1/2 small jalapeño pepper, seeded and minced

2 teaspoons freshly squeezed lime juice, plus the juice of half a lime, divided

1/2 teaspoon fine sea salt, divided

1-pound ball pizza dough, homemade (pages 17-19) or store-bought

2 ripe avocados

1/4 cup sliced black olives (optional)

1/2 cup crumbled feta cheese or queso blanco

USE WHOLE-WHEAT PIZZA DOUGH (PAGE 18) AND LOW-FAT CHEESE.

INSTRUCTIONS

BAKING STONE/STEEL: Place your baking stone on the middle rack of the oven and preheat to 500°F for at least 30 minutes. Dust a pizza peel or inverted baking sheet with cornmeal or flour.

BAKING SHEET: Preheat the oven to 500°F with a rack in the middle position. Lightly coat a heavy-duty, rimmed baking sheet with olive oil.

1. In a small bowl, make the pico de gallo by mixing together the tomato, cilantro, red onion, jalapeño, 2 teaspoons lime juice, and 1/4 teaspoon of the salt. Set aside.

2. Stretch or roll the dough into a 12-inch disk and place it on the prepared pizza peel or baking sheet.

3. Brush the dough with olive oil, then shimmy it onto the hot baking stone or transfer the baking sheet to the oven.

4. Bake just until the crust is golden (5 to 7 minutes on the baking stone; 10 to 12 minutes on the baking sheet).

5. Remove the crust from the oven and set it aside while you make the guacamole.

6. Halve and pit the avocados and scoop the flesh into a medium bowl. Add the juice of half a lime and the remaining 1/4 teaspoon of salt and mash it all together with a fork or a potato masher until smooth. Taste and add more salt as desired.

7. Scoop the guacamole onto the pizza crust and spread it out evenly, leaving a 1/2-inch border of crust all around.

8. Using a slotted spoon, scatter on the pico de gallo, and, if you prefer them, add the sliced olives and sprinkle the cheese on top. Slice and serve.

SHAKSHUKA PIZZA

MAKES ONE
12-INCH PIZZA

Shakshuka is a Middle Eastern dish of eggs simmered in spicy tomato-red pepper sauce. This pizzafied version, with smoky, baked eggs, will knock you on your shell!

INGREDIENTS

Extra-virgin olive oil for greasing

1-pound ball pizza dough, homemade (pages 17-19) or store-bought

2/3 cup New York-Style Pizza Sauce (page 23)

1 teaspoon smoked paprika

4 large eggs

1/2 cup chopped roasted red peppers

1/2 cup grated Parmesan cheese

Fine sea salt and freshly ground black pepper

1 tablespoon finely chopped fresh flat-leaf parsley

INSTRUCTIONS

1. Preheat the oven to 500°F with a rack in the middle position. Lightly coat a heavy-duty, rimmed baking sheet with olive oil.

2. Stretch or roll the dough into a 12-inch disk and place it on the prepared baking sheet.

3. In a small bowl, stir together the pizza sauce and paprika.

4. Crack the eggs into separate small prep bowls or ramekins.

5. Spread the sauce over the dough, leaving a ½-inch border of dough all around.

6. Scatter on the roasted red peppers, and then carefully slide the eggs onto the pizza an inch or two inside the edge, evenly distributed.

7. Sprinkle with the Parmesan cheese and season with a little salt and pepper.

8. Transfer the baking sheet to the oven and bake until the crust is golden, the egg whites are set, and the yolks are still a little squishy (10 to 15 minutes).

9. Remove the pizza from the oven. Let it rest for 5 minutes, then sprinkle with the parsley; slice and serve.

Lighten It Up, DUDE!

USE WHOLE-WHEAT PIZZA DOUGH (PAGE 18).

THE BLT

MAKES ONE 12-INCH PIZZA

What happens when the world's most awesome food meets a killer sandwich? This totally tubular pie, natch!

INGREDIENTS

Cornmeal or flour for dusting

Extra-virgin olive oil for brushing and greasing

4 slices thick-cut bacon, chopped

1-pound ball pizza dough, homemade (pages 17-19) or store-bought

5 slices American cheese

2 medium (or 1 large) ripe tomatoes, thinly sliced

Fine sea salt

1/4 cup mayonnaise

1/2 heaping cup loosely packed shredded Bibb lettuce

Lighten It Up, DUDE! USE WHOLE-WHEAT PIZZA DOUGH (PAGE 18), TURKEY OR VEGAN BACON, LOW-FAT CHEESE, AND LOW-FAT MAYONNAISE.

DID YOU KNOW, BRO? ACCORDING TO A REPORT PUBLISHED BY THE USDA IN 2014, ABOUT 13 PERCENT OF AMERICANS EAT PIZZA ON ANY GIVEN DAY. THAT'S MORE THAN 41 MILLION PEOPLE!

INSTRUCTIONS

BAKING STONE/STEEL: Place your baking stone on the middle rack of the oven and preheat to 500°F for at least 30 minutes, then turn the oven to broil. Dust a pizza peel or inverted baking sheet with cornmeal or flour.

BAKING SHEET: Preheat the oven to 500°F with a rack in the middle position. Lightly coat a heavy-duty, rimmed baking sheet with olive oil.

1. Cook the bacon in a medium skillet over medium heat for 5 to 7 minutes, stirring every minute or two until it begins to crisp at the edges. Remove the skillet from the heat and transfer the bacon to a paper towel–lined plate to drain.

2. Stretch or roll the dough into a 12-inch disk and place it on the prepared pizza peel or baking sheet.

3. Brush the dough lightly with oil, then tile on the cheese, followed by the tomato slices. Sprinkle the bacon over top.

4. Shimmy the dough from the peel to the hot baking stone or transfer the baking sheet to the oven.

5. Bake until the crust is golden and the cheese begins to brown in spots (6 to 8 minutes on the baking stone; 10 to 15 minutes on the baking sheet).

6. Remove the pizza from the oven and let it rest for 5 minutes, then sprinkle with a pinch of salt.

7. Scoop the mayonnaise into a resealable plastic bag and snip off the tip of one bottom corner.

8. Pipe the mayo in a zigzag pattern over the pizza and scatter the lettuce on top. Slice and serve.

MIGHTY MEATBALL AND SAUERKRAUT PIZZA

The Reuben can be found on just about every NYC deli menu. The classic is made with corned beef, sauerkraut, Swiss cheese, and Thousand Island or Russian dressing. The Turtles substitute turkey meatballs for the beef, since they won't dry out in the oven, and pizza for bread because they're on the ninja diet, bro!

INGREDIENTS

MEATBALLS

½ cup plain breadcrumbs

2 tablespoons finely grated Parmesan

¼ cup chopped fresh flat-leaf parsley, plus more for garnish

½ small yellow onion, finely grated or minced

1 large garlic clove, finely grated or minced

1 tablespoon ketchup

1 large egg, whisked

½ teaspoon salt

½ teaspoon freshly ground black pepper

1 pound ground turkey

SAUCE

½ cup sour cream

3 tablespoons ketchup

2 tablespoons pickle relish

INSTRUCTIONS

PIZZA

Cornmeal or flour for dusting

Extra-virgin olive oil for greasing

1-pound ball pizza dough, homemade (pages 17–19) or store-bought

¾ cup drained sauerkraut

¾ cup shredded Swiss cheese

Fine sea salt

Freshly ground black pepper

1 tablespoon chopped fresh parsley

MAKES ONE
12-INCH PIZZA

INSTRUCTIONS

Preheat the oven to 400°F with your baking steel/stone (if using) in the center position. Line a heavy-duty, rimmed baking sheet with parchment or aluminum foil.

TO MAKE THE MEATBALLS

1. In a large bowl, combine the breadcrumbs, Parmesan, parsley, onion, garlic, ketchup, egg, salt, and pepper.

2. Mix well using a wooden spoon, then add the turkey and mix with your hands just until all the ingredients are fully incorporated.

3. Scoop out 1 tablespoon of the mixture and roll it into a ball with your hands. Repeat with the rest of the mixture. You should have about 24 meatballs.

4. Place the meatballs on the prepared baking sheet, spacing them about 1 inch apart. Drizzle them with olive oil and bake for 15 minutes or until cooked through.

5. Remove the baking sheet from the oven and set the meatballs aside to cool.

6. When they are cool enough to handle, cut eight of the meatballs in half and place the rest of them in an airtight container to be eaten later in the week. (These meatballs are delicious with marinara sauce or pesto over pasta. They will keep for 3 to 5 days in the refrigerator and up to 6 months in the freezer.)

TO ASSEMBLE

1. Increase the oven temperature to 500°F.

2. If you're using a baking stone or steel, dust a pizza peel or inverted baking sheet with cornmeal or flour. If you're using the same baking sheet to bake your pizza, remove the parchment or foil and rub the baking sheet lightly with olive oil.

3. If you're using a baking stone or steel, turn the oven to broil.

4. Stretch or roll the dough into a 12-inch disk and place it on the prepared pizza peel or baking sheet.

5. In a small bowl, stir together the sour cream, ketchup, and relish.

6. Spread two heaping tablespoons of the sauce onto the dough, then arrange the meatball halves on top, cut-sides down.

7. Sprinkle on the sauerkraut and cheese and season with salt and pepper.

8. Shimmy the dough from the peel to the hot baking stone or transfer the baking sheet to the oven.

9. Bake until the crust is golden and the cheese is just beginning to brown in spots (6 to 8 minutes on the baking stone; 10 to 15 minutes on the baking sheet).

10. Remove the pizza from the oven and let it rest for 5 minutes, then sprinkle with the parsley. Slice and serve with the rest of the sauce for dipping.

Lighten It Up, DUDE!

USE WHOLE-WHEAT PIZZA DOUGH (PAGE 18), WHOLE-WHEAT BREADCRUMBS, SALT-FREE KETCHUP, LOW-FAT MILK, LOW-FAT CHEESE, AND PLAIN LOW-FAT YOGURT INSTEAD OF THE SOUR CREAM.

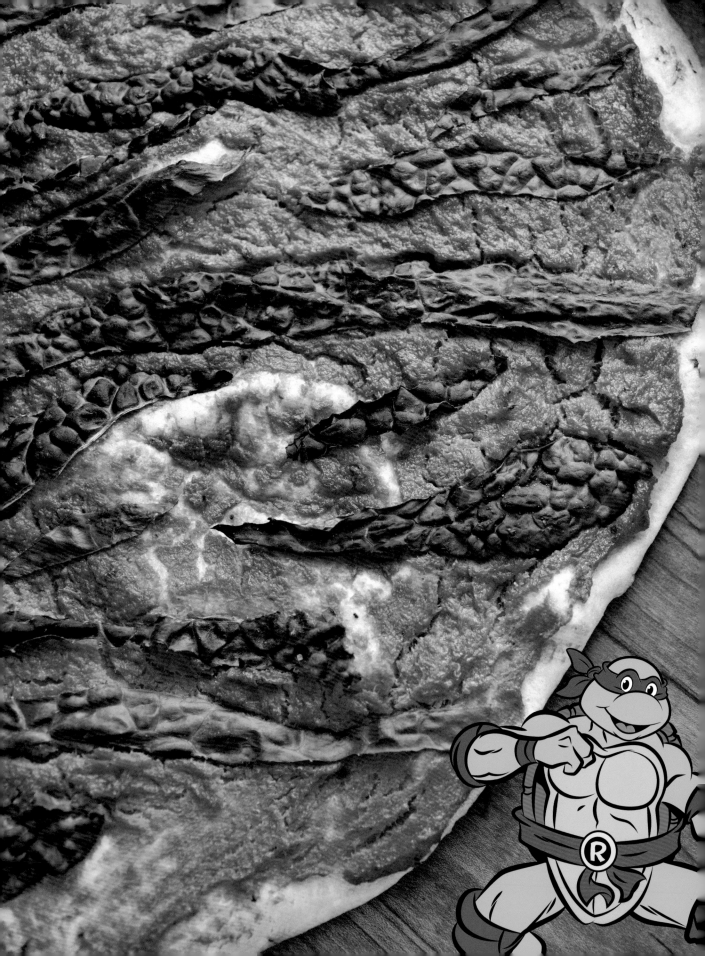

LEO'S KATANA SLASHES

MAKES ONE
12-INCH PIZZA

The twin swords wielded by Leonardo can intimidate even the most fearsome enemy. This is his homage to his trusty weapons, and it packs a more wholesome punch.

INGREDIENTS

1 small (2-pound) butternut squash, peeled, seeded, and cut into 1/2-inch cubes

1 tablespoon vegetable oil

Fine sea salt

Freshly ground black pepper

Cornmeal or flour for dusting

Extra-virgin olive oil for greasing

3 tablespoons unsweetened coconut milk

1 teaspoon grated fresh ginger

1 tablespoon soy sauce

1/4 teaspoon crushed red pepper flakes (optional)

1 pound ball pizza dough, homemade (pages 17-19) or store-bought

1 small bunch lacinato or dinosaur kale, ribs removed

Lighten It Up, DUDE!

USE WHOLE-WHEAT PIZZA DOUGH (PAGE 18) AND LOW-FAT COCONUT MILK.

INSTRUCTIONS

1. Preheat the oven to 450°F with your baking steel/stone (if using) in the center position. Line a heavy-duty, rimmed baking sheet with parchment or aluminum foil.

2. Spread the squash out in a single layer on the prepared baking sheet. Drizzle with the vegetable oil and season with salt and pepper.

3. Roast for 15 to 20 minutes until tender, stirring halfway through.

4. Remove the squash from the oven and set it aside to cool slightly. Increase the oven temperature to 500°F.

5. If you're using a baking stone or steel, dust a pizza peel or inverted baking sheet with cornmeal or flour. If you're using the same baking sheet to bake your pizza, remove the parchment or foil and rub the baking sheet lightly with olive oil.

6. When the squash is cool enough to handle, transfer it to the bowl of a food processor and add the coconut milk, ginger, and soy sauce. If you want a spicier taste, add the red pepper flakes to the mixture. Puree until smooth.

7. Stretch or roll the dough into a 12-inch disk and place it on the prepared pizza peel or baking sheet.

8. Scoop the butternut squash puree onto the dough and spread it out evenly, leaving a 1/2-inch border of dough all around. Using kitchen shears or a sharp paring knife, cut the kale leaves into strips. Press the kale strips onto the squash puree.

9. Shimmy the dough from the peel to the hot baking stone or transfer the baking sheet to the oven.

10. Bake for 8 to 15 minutes or until the crust is golden and the stripes are brown in spots.

11. Remove the pizza from the oven and let it rest for 5 minutes, then slice and serve.

MU SHU PORK PIE

MAKES ONE 12-INCH PIZZA

A staple on menus in Chinatown, mu shu pork is served with thin pancakes. But why have a pancake when you can have a pizza?

INGREDIENTS

Cornmeal or flour for dusting

Extra-virgin olive oil for greasing

1-pound ball pizza dough, homemade (pages 17–19) or store-bought

1 teaspoon plus 2 tablespoons vegetable oil, plus more for brushing

1 tablespoon soy sauce

½ cup hoisin sauce, divided

½ pound pork tenderloin, halved lengthwise, then thinly sliced

2 large eggs, beaten

½ small head savoy cabbage, cored and thinly sliced or shredded

4 ounces stemmed shiitake mushrooms, thinly sliced

1 large carrot, peeled and coarsely grated

2 scallions, white and light green parts thinly sliced

2 teaspoons grated fresh ginger

INSTRUCTIONS

BAKING STONE/STEEL: Place your baking stone on the middle rack of the oven and preheat to 500°F for at least 30 minutes, then turn the oven to broil. Dust a pizza peel or inverted baking sheet with cornmeal or flour.

BAKING SHEET: Preheat the oven to 500°F with a rack in the middle position. Lightly coat a heavy-duty, rimmed baking sheet with olive oil.

1. Stretch or roll the dough into a 12-inch disk and place it on the prepared pizza peel or baking sheet. Brush the dough with vegetable oil.

2. Shimmy the dough from the peel to the hot baking stone or transfer the baking sheet to the oven. Bake just until the crust is golden (5 to 7 minutes on the baking stone; 10 to 12 minutes on the baking sheet). Remove the crust from the oven and set it aside.

3. In a medium bowl, whisk together the soy sauce and ¼ cup of the hoisin sauce. Add the pork and toss to coat, then cover the bowl with plastic wrap and set it aside.

4. Heat 1 teaspoon of the oil in a large, nonstick skillet over medium heat. Add the eggs and let them cook for 1 to 2 minutes without stirring, just until set. Transfer the eggs to a cutting board and let them cool. Once the eggs are cool enough to handle, roll them up and cut into thin strips.

5. Wipe and return the skillet to the stove over high heat. Add 1 tablespoon of oil to the skillet. Using tongs, transfer the pork to the hot skillet, reserving its marinade. Stir-fry for 4 to 5 minutes or until cooked through. Immediately transfer the pork to a plate, along with any accumulated juices.

6. Add the remaining tablespoon of oil to the skillet and return it to high heat. When the oil is hot and begins to shimmer, add the cabbage, mushrooms, carrot, and scallions. Stir-fry for 5 minutes or until the vegetables are soft, then toss in the ginger and stir-fry for another 30 seconds.

7. Add the pork with its juices, the reserved marinade, and the eggs and stir-fry for another 2 minutes.

8. Using a slotted spoon, add the mu shu pork onto the pizza crust and drizzle with the remaining hoisin sauce. Slice and serve.

Lighten It Up, DUDE! USE WHOLE-WHEAT PIZZA DOUGH (PAGE 18) AND LOW-SODIUM SOY SAUCE.

ANCHOVY PIZZA WITH EXTRA GARLIC

MAKES ONE 12-INCH PIZZA

Love 'em or hate 'em, anchovies on pizza are a thing. Mikey has an undying love for the little fish, even though his brothers aren't on board. With lots of mellow, roasted garlic and salty cheese, this recipe is sure to bring out the anchovy lover (or hater) in everyone!

INGREDIENTS

Cornmeal or flour for dusting

Extra-virgin olive oil for brushing, greasing, and drizzling

1-pound ball pizza dough, homemade (pages 17-19) or store-bought

Cloves from 1 head roasted garlic (page 29), mashed

Salt and freshly ground black pepper

8 to 10 anchovy fillets packed in oil

3/4 cup shredded Manchego cheese

1/4 cup grated Parmesan cheese

1 tablespoon chopped fresh parsley

Lighten It Up, DUDE! USE WHOLE-WHEAT PIZZA DOUGH (PAGE 18) AND LOW-FAT CHEESE.

INSTRUCTIONS

BAKING STONE/STEEL: Place your baking stone on the middle rack of the oven and preheat to 500°F for at least 30 minutes, then turn the oven to broil. Dust a pizza peel or inverted baking sheet with cornmeal or flour.

BAKING SHEET: Preheat the oven to 500°F with a rack in the middle position. Lightly coat a heavy-duty, rimmed baking sheet with olive oil.

1. Stretch or roll the dough into a 12-inch disk and place it on the prepared pizza peel or baking sheet.

2. Brush the dough with olive oil. Scoop the mashed roasted garlic onto the dough and spread it out evenly. Season with salt and pepper.

3. Arrange the anchovy fillets on top and sprinkle on the Manchego and Parmesan.

4. Shimmy the dough from the peel to the hot baking stone or transfer the baking sheet to the oven.

5. Bake until the crust is golden and the cheese begins to brown in spots (6 to 8 minutes on the baking stone; 10 to 15 minutes on the baking sheet).

6. Remove the pizza from the oven and let it rest for 5 minutes. Sprinkle on the parsley, and give the pizza a little drizzle of olive oil. Slice and serve.

THE APRIL O'NEIL

MAKES ONE 12-INCH PIZZA

The bright orange color of this pizza is nearly the same shade as April's hair. With sweet potatoes and spicy mustard, this pie is unique and fierce . . . just like April!

INGREDIENTS

Cornmeal or flour for dusting

Extra-virgin olive oil for greasing

1 large parsnip, peeled and cut into 1-inch pieces

1 medium sweet potato, peeled and cut into 1-inch pieces

1 tablespoon plus 1 teaspoon whole or low-fat milk

1 ½ teaspoons Dijon mustard

1 teaspoon honey

¼ teaspoon salt

Freshly ground black pepper

1 teaspoon finely chopped fresh sage, plus more for garnish

1-pound ball pizza dough, homemade (pages 17-19) or store-bought

¾ cup extra-sharp cheddar cheese

Lighten It Up, DUDE!

USE WHOLE-WHEAT PIZZA DOUGH (PAGE 18) AND LOW-FAT COCONUT MILK.

INSTRUCTIONS

BAKING STONE/STEEL: Place your baking stone on the middle rack of the oven and preheat to 500°F for at least 30 minutes, then turn the oven to broil. Dust a pizza peel or inverted baking sheet with cornmeal or flour.

BAKING SHEET: Preheat the oven to 500°F with a rack in the middle position. Lightly coat a heavy-duty, rimmed baking sheet with olive oil.

1. Bring a large pot of water to a boil and drop in the parsnip and sweet potato.

2. Bring the water back to a boil and cook for 20 minutes, uncovered, until the vegetables are very tender when pierced with a fork. Drain and transfer the vegetables to the bowl of a food processor.

3. Puree until smooth, and then add the milk, mustard, honey, salt, and a few grinds of pepper. Process until the mixture is uniform in color, adding a little more milk if it seems too thick to spread on the pizza dough. Stir in the sage and season to taste with more salt and pepper if needed.

4. Stretch or roll the dough into a 12-inch disk and place it on the prepared pizza peel or baking sheet.

5. Spoon the puree onto the dough and spread it evenly, leaving a ½-inch border all around. Sprinkle the cheese over the top.

6. Shimmy the dough from the peel to the hot baking stone or transfer the baking sheet to the oven.

7. Bake until the crust is golden and the cheese begins to brown in spots (6 to 10 minutes on the baking stone; 10 to 15 minutes on the baking sheet).

8. Remove the pizza from the oven and let it rest for 5 minutes, then sprinkle with the remaining chopped sage. Slice and serve.

SHREDDER'S REVENGE

MAKES ONE
12-INCH PIZZA

Shredder is one stressed-out bad guy. To unwind, he likes to shut himself in the kitchen and let his blades loose on whatever veggies he can find. This pizza is the delicious result of one of his more violent tantrums.

INGREDIENTS

Cornmeal or flour for dusting

Extra-virgin olive oil for greasing

1-pound ball pizza dough, homemade (pages 17-19) or store-bought

One 6- to 8-ounce chicken breast, cooked and shredded

½ cup buffalo hot sauce

1 medium carrot, peeled

1 stalk celery

½ medium red onion, peeled

½ cup chunky blue cheese dressing, plus more for drizzling

½ cup shredded Monterey Jack cheese

½ cup shredded low-moisture mozzarella

Freshly ground black pepper

2 scallions, white and light green parts finely chopped

INSTRUCTIONS

BAKING STONE/STEEL: Place your baking stone on the middle rack of the oven and preheat to 500°F for at least 30 minutes, then turn the oven to broil. Dust a pizza peel or inverted baking sheet with cornmeal or flour.

BAKING SHEET: Preheat the oven to 500°F with a rack in the middle position. Lightly coat a heavy-duty, rimmed baking sheet with olive oil.

1. Stretch or roll the dough into a 12-inch disk and place it on the prepared pizza peel or baking sheet.

2. Toss together the shredded chicken and buffalo sauce in a medium bowl.

3. Shred the carrot, celery, and onion with the coarse grating blade of a food processor. (Or grate them with the coarse side of a box grater.)

4. Spread the blue cheese dressing over the dough, leaving a ½-inch border all around.

5. Arrange the chicken on top, followed by the shredded vegetables, and finish with the cheeses. Season with a few grinds of black pepper.

6. Shimmy the dough from the peel to the hot baking stone or transfer the baking sheet to the oven.

7. Bake until the crust is golden and the cheese begins to brown in spots (6 to 8 minutes on the baking stone; 10 to 15 minutes on the baking sheet).

8. Remove the pizza from the oven and let it rest for 5 minutes, then sprinkle with the scallions and drizzle lightly with blue cheese dressing. Slice and serve.

Lighten It Up, **DUDE!** POACH THE CHICKEN. USE WHOLE-WHEAT PIZZA DOUGH (PAGE 18) AND LOW-FAT BLUE CHEESE DRESSING AND MOZZARELLA.

THE LEAN, MEAN, AND GREEN

MAKES ONE 12-INCH PIZZA

The Turtles always thought cheese-less pizza was a bogus idea . . . until Master Splinter whipped this one up, inspired by his Japanese heritage. Topped with crumbled tofu and crammed full of vibrant flavors, it satisfies all the requirements for a radical pie, and it's the perfect thing to serve when vegan friends come down to the lair.

INGREDIENTS

Cornmeal or flour for dusting

Extra-virgin olive oil for greasing

1 large head of broccoli, broken into bite-size florets, thick stems discarded or saved for another use

1-pound ball pizza dough, homemade (pages 17-19) or store-bought

Vegetable oil for brushing

1 large garlic clove, very thinly sliced

One 14-ounce container extra-firm tofu, drained, patted dry, and crumbled

Sesame oil

Soy sauce

Pinch of crushed red pepper flakes (optional)

Lighten It Up, DUDE! USE WHOLE-WHEAT PIZZA DOUGH (PAGE 18).

INSTRUCTIONS

BAKING STONE/STEEL: Place your baking stone on the middle rack of the oven and preheat to 500°F for at least 30 minutes, then turn the oven to broil. Dust a pizza peel or inverted baking sheet with cornmeal or flour.

BAKING SHEET: Preheat the oven to 500°F with a rack in the middle position. Lightly coat a heavy-duty, rimmed baking sheet with olive oil.

1. Bring a large pot of water to a boil. Fill a medium bowl with ice water and place it nearby.

2. Drop the broccoli into the boiling water and let it cook for 2 minutes, then use a slotted spoon to transfer the broccoli to the ice water to set its color and stop the cooking. Drain well.

3. Stretch or roll the dough into a 12-inch disk and place it on the prepared pizza peel or baking sheet. Brush the dough lightly with vegetable oil, then scatter on the sliced garlic, blanched broccoli, and crumbled tofu.

4. Drizzle a little sesame oil on top and sprinkle lightly with soy sauce. Shimmy the dough from the peel to the hot baking stone or transfer the baking sheet to the oven.

5. Bake until the crust is golden (6 to 8 minutes on the baking stone; 10 to 15 minutes on the baking sheet).

6. Remove the pizza from the oven and let it rest for 5 minutes, then finish with the crushed red pepper flakes (if using). Slice and serve.

TOTAL TUNA MELTDOWN

MAKES ONE
12-INCH PIZZA

It might not be pretty to look at, but after one bite, you won't be able to resist this giant open-face sandwich!

INGREDIENTS

Cornmeal or flour for dusting

Extra-virgin olive oil for brushing and greasing

Two 5-ounce cans of tuna packed in water, drained well

1 celery stalk, minced

¼ small red onion, minced

5 sweet gherkin pickles, minced

1 tablespoon chopped fresh flat-leaf parsley

⅓ cup mayonnaise

2 tablespoons Dijon mustard

Salt and freshly ground black pepper

1-pound ball pizza dough, homemade (pages 17-19) or store-bought

¾ cup shredded mild cheddar cheese

USE WHOLE-WHEAT PIZZA DOUGH (PAGE 18).

INSTRUCTIONS

BAKING STONE/STEEL: Place your baking stone on the middle rack of the oven and preheat to 500°F for at least 30 minutes. Dust a pizza peel or inverted baking sheet with cornmeal or flour.

BAKING SHEET: Preheat the oven to 500°F with a rack in the middle position. Lightly coat a heavy-duty, rimmed baking sheet with olive oil.

1. Dump the tuna into a medium bowl and break it up with a fork.

2. Add the celery, onion, pickles, parsley, mayonnaise, and mustard and mix well. Season to taste with salt and pepper.

3. Cover and refrigerate until needed.

4. Stretch or roll the dough into a 12-inch disk, then place it on the prepared pizza peel or baking sheet and brush it lightly with olive oil.

5. Shimmy the dough from the peel to the hot baking stone or transfer the baking sheet to the oven.

6. Bake just until the crust is golden (5 to 7 minutes on the baking stone; 10 to 12 minutes on the baking sheet). Remove the crust from the oven. If you're using a baking stone or steel, turn the oven to broil.

7. Spread the tuna salad onto the pizza crust, leaving a ½-inch border all around.

8. Sprinkle on the cheese.

9. Return the pizza to the oven and broil just until the cheese has melted and browned in spots (3 to 7 minutes).

10. Remove the pizza from the oven and let it rest for 5 minutes. Slice and serve.

PEPPERONI AND SWEET PICKLE PIE

MAKES ONE
12-INCH PIZZA

Pepperoni and pickles are the perfect mash-up of salty and sweet, chewy and crisp.
Wanna go all-out savory? Swap the bread-and-butter pickles for dill slices instead.
Then get ready to do serious damage to this delectable pie!

INGREDIENTS

Cornmeal or flour for dusting

Extra-virgin olive oil for greasing

1-pound ball pizza dough, homemade
(pages 17-19) or store-bought

⅔ cup New York-Style Pizza Sauce (page 23)

¾ cup shredded low-moisture mozzarella
cheese

22 to 24 pepperoni slices

½ to 1 cup bread-and-butter pickle chips

INSTRUCTIONS

BAKING STONE/STEEL: Place your baking stone on the middle
rack of the oven and preheat to 500°F for at least 30
minutes, then turn the oven to broil. Dust a pizza peel or
inverted baking sheet with cornmeal or flour.

BAKING SHEET: Preheat the oven to 500°F with a rack in the
middle position. Lightly coat a heavy-duty, rimmed baking
sheet with olive oil.

1. Stretch or roll the dough into a 12-inch disk and place it
   on the prepared pizza peel or baking sheet.

2. Spoon the sauce onto the dough and spread it out in an
   even layer, leaving a ½-inch border of dough all around.

3. Sprinkle on half of the cheese, then arrange the
   pepperoni and pickles on top. Finish with the
   remaining cheese.

4. Shimmy the dough from the peel to the hot baking stone
   or transfer the baking sheet to the oven.

5. Bake until the crust is golden and the cheese begins to
   brown in spots (6 to 10 minutes on the baking stone;
   10 to 15 minutes on the baking sheet).

6. Remove the pizza from the oven and let it rest for
   5 minutes, then slice and serve.

Lighten It Up.
DUDE!

USE WHOLE-WHEAT PIZZA
DOUGH (PAGE 18) AND
LOW-FAT MOZZARELLA.

CRAZY CORN AND BODACIOUS BEAN PIZZA

MAKES ONE 12-INCH PIZZA

Whoa, dude! This one's like a fiesta in your mouth! Make some extra black bean puree to use for taco night or as a dip for tortilla chips. It'll keep in an airtight container in the fridge for up to 3 days.

INGREDIENTS

Cornmeal or flour for dusting

2 tablespoons extra-virgin olive oil, plus more for greasing

One 15 1/2-ounce can black beans, drained and rinsed

1 garlic clove, crushed

1 teaspoon ground cumin

1 teaspoon freshly squeezed lime juice

1/2 teaspoon lime zest

2 tablespoons water

Big pinch of salt

1-pound ball pizza dough, homemade (pages 17-19) or store-bought

1 cup fresh or frozen and thawed corn kernels

3/4 cup shredded Monterey Jack cheese

1/4 cup crumbled feta cheese or queso fresco

1 tablespoon chopped fresh cilantro

INSTRUCTIONS

BAKING STONE/STEEL: Place your baking stone on the middle rack of the oven and preheat to 500°F for at least 30 minutes, then turn the oven to broil. Dust a pizza peel or inverted baking sheet with cornmeal or flour.

BAKING SHEET: Preheat the oven to 500°F with a rack in the middle position. Lightly coat a heavy-duty, rimmed baking sheet with olive oil.

1. Toss the black beans, garlic, cumin, lime juice and zest, olive oil, water, and salt into the bowl of a food processor and blend everything together until the mixture is smooth and uniform in color. Taste and add more salt if needed.

2. Stretch or roll the dough into a 12-inch disk and place it on the prepared pizza peel or baking sheet.

3. Scoop the black bean puree onto the dough and spread it out in an even layer, leaving a 1/2-inch border of dough all around.

4. Scatter on the corn, then the Jack cheese.

5. Shimmy the dough from the peel to the hot baking stone or transfer the baking sheet to the oven.

6. Bake until the crust is golden and the cheese begins to brown in spots (6 to 8 minutes on the baking stone; 10 to 15 minutes on the baking sheet).

7. Remove the pizza from the oven and let it rest for 5 minutes. Sprinkle on the feta cheese and cilantro, then slice and serve.

Lighten It Up, DUDE!

USE WHOLE-WHEAT PIZZA DOUGH (PAGE 18) AND LOW-FAT MOZZARELLA.

MASKED MUTATIONS

THOUGH THEY HAVE TRIED, THE TURTLES CANNOT LIVE BY EATING PIZZA ALONE . . . BUT THAT DOESN'T MEAN YOUR GRUB CAN'T HAVE PIZZA FLAVOR! GET READY FOR SOME RIGHTEOUS RIFFS ON THESE NONPIZZA FAVORITES:

THE POWER OF PIZZA WILL BE WITH YOU IN SPIRIT!

PIZZA POTSTICKERS

MAKES ABOUT 50 DUMPLINGS

A rad mash-up of Splinter's Asian heritage and his sons' love of pizza, these dumplings make the perfect snack for any party. They do take practice, however, so don't bug out if you tear a few wrappers on your first try.

INGREDIENTS

- 1 large or 2 medium garlic cloves, pressed or minced
- ¼ cup minced yellow or white onion
- 1 link (¼ pound) sweet Italian sausage, casing removed
- ½ cup finely chopped pepperoni (about 1 ½ ounces)
- ½ cup shredded low-moisture mozzarella cheese
- 1 teaspoon Italian seasoning blend
- ⅛ teaspoon salt
- ⅛ teaspoon freshly ground black pepper
- 1 package wonton wrappers, preferably circular
- 2 tablespoons vegetable oil, plus more as needed
- 1 cup No-Cook Tomato Sauce (page 21) or store-bought marinara for dipping

Lighten It Up, DUDE!

USE TURKEY OR VEGAN SAUSAGE AND LOW-FAT CHEESE, AND SKIP THE PEPPERONI.

INSTRUCTIONS

1. Combine the garlic, onion, sausage, pepperoni, mozzarella, Italian seasoning, salt, and pepper in a medium bowl and mix with your hands until everything is incorporated.

2. Set up your work station. Fill a small bowl with water and lay out a bunch of the wonton wrappers. Place a rimmed baking sheet nearby.

3. Scoop 1 teaspoon of filling onto the center of a wrapper. Dip your finger into the water, then use it to moisten the outside edge of a wonton wrapper. Bring both sides of the wonton wrapper up and press them together around the filling. Pleat the wrapper to give it a good seal.

4. Place the finished potsticker on the baking sheet, pleated-side up. Repeat with the remaining wonton wrappers and filling.

5. Heat a large saucepan or Dutch oven over medium heat. Add 2 tablespoons of vegetable oil and swirl to coat the bottom of the pan. When the oil begins to shimmer (but not smoke!), place the potstickers carefully in the pan, pleated-sides up, spacing them a little bit apart. (You will probably have to cook the potstickers in batches.)

6. Cook uncovered for 3 to 5 minutes or until the potstickers are browned on the bottom, then pour in ¼ cup of water and immediately cover the pan.

7. Let the potstickers steam for 2 minutes, then lift the lid and check them for doneness. The filling should feel firm. If you're not sure whether or not they are done, cut one open and check that the filling is cooked through.

8. When the potstickers are done steaming, remove the lid and cook for 2 more minutes or until all the water has evaporated. Remove the potstickers from the pan, add 2 more tablespoons of oil, and repeat with the remaining uncooked potstickers.

9. Serve hot with pizza sauce for dipping.

BIG-CITY BURGERS

MAKES 4 BURGERS

Keeping the streets of NYC safe is a big job. And big-city heroes like the Turtles need a big-city burger! Since there's always mozzarella, pepperoni, and pizza sauce in the Turtle Lair fridge, even burger night is bound to include some pizza flavor.

INGREDIENTS

¹/₄ cup finely diced pepperoni (about 1 ounce)

1 tablespoon finely chopped black olives

2 teaspoons Italian seasoning blend

1 pound lean ground beef

Salt and freshly ground black pepper

Extra-virgin olive oil for brushing

¹/₂ to 1 cup No-Cook Tomato Sauce (page 21)

1 cup shredded low-moisture mozzarella

4 burger buns, split and toasted

Optional toppings: sautéed mushrooms, sliced olives, banana peppers, caramelized onions, or anything else you like

Lighten It Up, DUDE! SKIP THE PEPPERONI, SWAP OUT THE GROUND BEEF FOR GROUND TURKEY OR CHICKEN, AND USE LOW-FAT MOZZARELLA AND WHOLE-WHEAT BUNS.

INSTRUCTIONS

1. In a large bowl, toss together the pepperoni, olives, and Italian seasoning.

2. Crumble in the ground beef and mix gently with your hands just until everything is incorporated. Too much mixing makes for tough, dry burgers.

3. Divide the mixture into four equal portions and gently shape each into a ¾-inch-thick patty. Use your thumb to make a deep impression in the center of each one.

4. Season both sides of the patties generously with salt and pepper.

5. Place a large cast-iron skillet over medium-high heat until a droplet of water fizzles and evaporates in a few seconds. Brush the burgers on both sides with olive oil and place them in the skillet, indented sides up.

6. Cook for 3 to 4 minutes without disturbing the burgers, and then flip.

7. Scoop a spoonful of sauce onto each burger and top with a handful of mozzarella.

8. Cover the skillet or tent the burgers with foil and cook for 3 more minutes or until the cheese has melted.

9. Remove the finished burgers from the grill.

10. Spoon some extra sauce onto each bottom bun and place a burger on top.

11. Spoon a little more sauce on top of each burger and serve immediately with the extra toppings of your choice.

MASTER SPLINTER'S SPINACH CALZONES

MAKES 4 CALZONES

Part of Splinter's job as father and sensei is keeping his sons warrior-ready! These veggie powerhouses are perfect to eat now or later. Just whip up a double batch, let the extras cool to room temperature, then wrap them tightly in plastic and freeze. To reheat, defrost them in the fridge, then bake at 300°F until hot.

INGREDIENTS

2 teaspoons extra-virgin olive oil, plus more for greasing and brushing

1 small yellow onion, finely diced

2 large garlic cloves, minced or pressed

One 8-ounce bag baby spinach

3/4 cup ricotta cheese

Fine sea salt and freshly ground black pepper

1-pound ball pizza dough, homemade (pages 17-19) or store-bought

1/2 cup No-Cook Tomato Sauce (page 21)

Lighten It Up, DUDE!

USE WHOLE-WHEAT PIZZA DOUGH (PAGE 18) AND LOW-FAT RICOTTA.

INSTRUCTIONS

1. Position racks in the top and bottom thirds of the oven and preheat to 450°F. Rub two heavy-duty, rimmed baking sheets with a little olive oil.

2. Heat the oil in a medium skillet over medium heat. Add the onion and cook for about 5 minutes until it softens and just begins to brown, stirring constantly.

3. Toss in the garlic, then the spinach, and stir until the spinach has wilted, about 3 minutes.

4. Remove skillet from heat. Drain any excess liquid from the skillet and stir in the ricotta. Taste and season with salt and pepper as desired.

5. Place the dough on a well-floured work surface and divide it into four equal pieces. Roll each piece into a 6- or 7-inch circle.

6. Spread 2 tablespoons of pizza sauce on the bottom third of each dough circle, leaving a 1-inch border around the edge.

7. Spoon about ¼ cup of the spinach-ricotta mixture on top of the sauce on each calzone and spread it out just a little.

8. Fold the top part of the dough over the filling and pinch the edges together or roll and press them up to seal.

9. Place the calzones on the prepared baking sheets and brush them with oil. Using a knife, cut two or three short slits in the top of each calzone to allow steam to escape during cooking.

10. Bake for 15 minutes, then switch the baking sheets and bake for another 15 minutes or until the crust is golden brown and the cheese is bubbly.

11. Remove the calzones from the oven and let them cool for at least 5 minutes before serving.

COWABUNGA BOATS

MAKES 4 ZUCCHINI BOATS

Ride the wave to pizza town with these zucchini boats stuffed with sausage, olives, pepperoni, pizza sauce, and oozy mozzarella.

INGREDIENTS

1 teaspoon extra-virgin olive oil, plus more for greasing

2 medium zucchinis, halved lengthwise

2 links (½ pound) sweet or hot Italian sausage, casings removed

¼ cup sliced black olives

¼ cup finely diced pepperoni (about 1 ounce)

8 tablespoons No-Cook Tomato Sauce (page 21) or store-bought marinara

1 cup shredded low-moisture mozzarella cheese

Salt and freshly ground black pepper

1 tablespoon chopped fresh oregano

INSTRUCTIONS

1. Preheat the oven to 400°F. Coat a large baking dish lightly with olive oil.

2. Scoop out the flesh from the zucchini halves, making four boats.

3. Chop the zucchini flesh and set it aside.

4. Place the boats cut-side up in a baking dish.

5. Heat the teaspoon of oil in a small skillet over medium heat and crumble in the sausage. Cook, breaking it up with a wooden spoon until the sausage is no longer pink (about 5 minutes).

6. Toss in ¾ cup of the chopped zucchini flesh and sauté until tender, 3 to 5 more minutes.

7. Remove the pan from the heat. Discard the remaining zucchini flesh or save it for a later use.

8. Divide the sausage mixture evenly among the zucchini boats, then top each boat with 1 tablespoon black olives, 1 tablespoon pepperoni, 2 tablespoons sauce, and ¼ cup cheese. Season to taste with salt and pepper.

9. Bake for 15 to 20 minutes or until the zucchini is tender and the cheese is melted. Remove the boats from the oven, sprinkle with oregano, and serve warm.

Lighten It Up, DUDE!

SKIP THE PEPPERONI AND USE TURKEY OR VEGAN SAUSAGE AND LOW-FAT MOZZARELLA.

BEBOP POPCORN

MAKES ABOUT 8 CUPS

Bebop might have been mutated into a human-warthog, but it doesn't mean he eats like a pig! This classed-up popcorn has a punch of pizza flavor that will knock you on your shell.

INGREDIENTS

4 tablespoons unsalted butter

1 small garlic clove, pressed or very finely minced

2 heaping tablespoons finely minced oil-packed sun-dried tomatoes

Heaping 1/3 cup popcorn kernels

1 1/2 tablespoons grapeseed or sunflower oil

2 to 3 tablespoons finely grated Parmesan cheese

3/4 teaspoon dried basil

3/4 teaspoon dried oregano

1/2 teaspoon fine sea salt

INSTRUCTIONS

1. Melt the butter in a small saucepan over medium heat. Add the garlic and cook, stirring constantly for 30 seconds to 1 minute, just until fragrant.

2. Add the sun-dried tomatoes. Stir well, cover, and keep warm over low heat.

3. Place the popcorn kernels and oil in a large saucepan or Dutch oven and toss well to coat the kernels in the oil. Cover the pan and set it over medium heat.

4. When you hear the kernels begin to pop, give the pan a good shake. Continue to cook, shaking frequently, until the popping slows to 3 to 4 seconds between pops.

5. Dump the popcorn into a large bowl.

6. Drizzle the warm butter mixture over the popcorn and add the Parmesan cheese, basil, oregano, and salt. Toss well before serving.

Lighten It Up, DUDE!

SKIP THE PARMESAN AND SALT.

ROCKSTEADY ROLLS

MAKES 12 ROLLS

These rolls will satisfy the mightiest of appetites—even half-rhino Rocksteady's. A bad guy's recipe never tasted so good.

INGREDIENTS

1-pound ball pizza dough, homemade (pages 17-19) or store-bought

Extra-virgin olive oil for brushing

1/2 cup No-Cook Tomato Sauce (page 21) or store-bought marinara, plus extra for dipping

2/3 cup shredded low-moisture mozzarella cheese

1/4 cup sliced black olives

2 tablespoons chopped fresh basil

30 pepperoni slices

Fine sea salt and freshly ground black pepper

1/2 cup grated Parmesan cheese

INSTRUCTIONS

1. Line a heavy-duty, rimmed baking sheet with parchment paper.

2. On a lightly floured work surface, roll out the dough into a 9- by 12-inch rectangle.

3. Brush the dough with a little olive oil, then spread the sauce evenly on top, leaving a 1/2-inch border of dough all around.

4. Sprinkle on the mozzarella, olives, and basil and top with the pepperoni slices. Season with a little salt and pepper.

5. Starting from one of the long sides, roll the rectangle into a long, tight log.

6. Place the log on the prepared baking sheet and refrigerate for at least 20 minutes or until chilled through.

7. Preheat the oven to 375°F.

8. Remove the log from the fridge and cut it crosswise into twelve 1-inch-thick rolls. Arrange the rolls cut-side up on the baking sheet. (It's okay if they touch.)

9. Sprinkle the rolls with the Parmesan cheese and bake for 20 to 30 minutes or until the cheese has melted and the crust is golden brown.

10. Remove the rolls from the oven and let them cool for 5 minutes. Serve warm with extra pizza sauce for dipping.

Lighten It Up, DUDE!

USE WHOLE-WHEAT PIZZA DOUGH (PAGE 18) AND LOW-FAT MOZZARELLA AND SKIP THE PEPPERONI.

PIZZA RAMEN SOUP

MAKES 4 SERVINGS

Comfort food means different things to different people. To Splinter, it's ramen, the traditional Japanese noodle soup. But for his sons, it's pizza that gets them stoked. This dish is East meets West and tradition meets new kid on the block—all in one tasty bowl!

INGREDIENTS

½ cup (about 2 ounces) finely diced pepperoni

1 medium green bell pepper, halved, seeded, and chopped

½ medium yellow onion, chopped

8 ounces sliced white mushrooms

½ teaspoon fine sea salt

2 garlic cloves, minced or pressed

Freshly ground black pepper

1 quart low-sodium chicken or vegetable broth

One 15-ounce can pizza sauce

3 tablespoons grated Parmesan cheese

One 3 ½-ounce package unflavored instant ramen noodles

1 tablespoon chopped fresh oregano

2 ounces fresh mozzarella cheese, cubed

INSTRUCTIONS

1. Place a large pot over medium-high heat and add the pepperoni. Cook until it renders its fat and crisps up a little, about 3 minutes. Using a slotted spoon, transfer the pepperoni to a plate.

2. Reduce the heat to medium and add the bell pepper, onion, mushrooms, and salt. Cook, stirring frequently, until the vegetables are tender and beginning to brown (5 to 7 minutes).

3. Add the garlic and stir for 30 seconds, then give it a few grinds of black pepper.

4. Pour in the broth and pizza sauce and add the Parmesan cheese. Stir well.

5. Bring the soup to a boil, reduce the heat to medium low, and cover the pot. Simmer for 10 minutes, then add the ramen noodles and pepperoni.

6. Cook for 5 to 7 more minutes, stirring occasionally, until the ramen noodles are cooked through.

7. Stir in the oregano, taste, and adjust the seasonings with more salt and pepper as needed.

8. Divide the soup among four bowls, top with the cubed mozzarella, and serve immediately.

Lighten It Up, DUDE!

SKIP THE PEPPERONI AND USE SALT-FREE PIZZA SAUCE AND WHOLE-WHEAT PASTA INSTEAD OF THE RAMEN NOODLES.

PESTO PIZZA POCKETS

MAKES 4 SANDWICHES

When the Turtles have to leave the lair in a hurry, Master Splinter packs them each a pizza pocket to eat on the go. These are made with pesto, pancetta, fresh tomato, and arugula, but you can use whatever pizza ingredients you have in the fridge.

INGREDIENTS

4 tablespoons pesto, homemade (page 27) or store-bought

4 pita pockets

8 thin slices pancetta, chopped

1 medium vine-ripened tomato, thinly sliced

4 to 6 ounces fresh mozzarella, thinly sliced

1 packed cup baby arugula

Extra-virgin olive oil for drizzling

Salt and freshly ground black pepper

INSTRUCTIONS

1. Spread ¼ tablespoon of pesto inside each pita pocket. Tuck one quarter of the chopped pancetta, one or two tomato slices, and a slice or two of mozzarella inside.

2. Divide the arugula among the pockets and give each a drizzle of olive oil.

3. Season lightly with salt and pepper before serving.

Lighten It Up, DUDE!

USE WHOLE-WHEAT PITA POCKETS AND LOW-FAT CHEESE.

RAPH'S WAFFLES

MAKES 2 WAFFLES

When Raphael needs a cure for the midnight munchies, he reaches for one of these bad boys. They're the perfect thing to chow down on while watching *Bugzilla vs. the Snail Monster* or an *Ace Duck* movie marathon. **PRO TIP:** Double the recipe if you've got a Michelangelo in the house!

INGREDIENTS

- 1-pound ball pizza dough, homemade (pages 17-19) or store-bought
- 1/3 cup No-Cook Tomato Sauce (page 21) or store-bought marinara, plus more for dipping
- 4 thin slices pancetta
- 1/2 cup shredded low-moisture mozzarella cheese
- Dried oregano
- Extra-virgin olive oil for brushing
- Nonstick cooking spray for greasing

Lighten It Up, DUDE!

USE WHOLE-WHEAT PIZZA DOUGH (PAGE 18) AND LOW-FAT MOZZARELLA.

DID YOU KNOW, BRO?
PEOPLE IN THE UNITED STATES SPEND ABOUT $38 BILLION ON PIZZA EVERY YEAR. THAT'S A LOT OF DOUGH!

INSTRUCTIONS

1. Preheat a Belgian or other 1-inch-deep waffle iron on the medium-high setting.

2. Cut the ball of dough into four equal-size pieces. Set two pieces aside and cover them with a damp dish towel.

3. On a floured work surface, roll or stretch out the first two dough pieces to fit just inside the mold of your waffle maker.

4. Spread a spoonful of marinara sauce onto one of the rolled or stretched-out dough disks and spread it out, leaving a 1-inch border of dough all around.

5. Place two slices of pancetta on top of the sauce, then half of the cheese. Sprinkle with oregano.

6. Brush the exposed border of dough with olive oil, and then brush some more olive oil around the perimeter of the second rolled or stretched out dough disk. Invert the naked dough disk onto the dressed one and pinch around the edges to seal. Brush the top with olive oil.

7. Open your waffle iron (it should be really hot by now) and coat it with nonstick cooking spray. Carefully invert the pizza dough packet onto the iron, oiled side down, and brush the top with more olive oil.

8. Close the waffle iron and cook for 3 to 5 minutes or until the crust is golden brown but still springy to the touch. (This part is loud and messy, as some of the cheese and sauce will bubble and ooze out of the waffle iron.)

9. When the waffle is done, remove it from the iron and repeat with the remaining dough pieces and fillings.

10. To serve, fill a ramekin or small bowl with some of the marinara sauce. Cut the waffles into wedges or sticks and serve them with the sauce for dipping.

TURTLE POWER PIZZA SALAD

MAKES 6 TO 8 SERVINGS

Pizza salad? Whoa, bro! Now we're talking. Add any mix of your favorite toppings to this super-easy salad. You could even skip the dressing and use sun-dried tomato pesto or Any-Herb Pesto (page 27), too.

INGREDIENTS

- 8 ounces uncooked fusilli pasta
- 1 pint cherry tomatoes, halved or quartered
- 1 medium green bell pepper, seeded and diced
- 1/2 cup sliced scallions (white and light green parts only)
- 1/2 cup sliced black olives
- 2/3 cup finely diced pepperoni (about 2 ounces)
- 1 cup diced low-moisture mozzarella cheese
- 1/4 cup grated Parmesan cheese
- Handful of fresh basil leaves, torn or roughly chopped
- 1/2 cup extra-virgin olive oil
- 1/4 cup red wine vinegar
- 1 teaspoon salt-free Italian seasoning blend
- 1/2 teaspoon garlic powder
- 1/2 teaspoon fine sea salt
- 1/4 teaspoon freshly ground black pepper

INSTRUCTIONS

1. Bring a large pot of water to a boil and cook the pasta to al dente, according to the package directions.

2. Drain immediately and rinse the pasta under cold running water. Drain well and transfer the pasta to a large bowl.

3. Add the tomatoes, green pepper, scallions, olives, pepperoni, mozzarella, Parmesan, and basil. Toss gently until everything is evenly distributed.

4. In a small bowl, whisk together the oil, vinegar, Italian seasoning, garlic powder, salt, and black pepper.

5. Drizzle the dressing over the salad and toss well. Taste and adjust seasonings as desired.

Lighten It Up, DUDE!

USE WHOLE-WHEAT PASTA AND LOW-FAT MOZZARELLA AND SKIP THE PEPPERONI OR SWAP IT WITH CUBED POACHED CHICKEN.

GREEN OOZE SMOOTHIE

MAKES 2 SERVINGS

Don't worry—there's no mutagen in this neon-green smoothie. But if you start your day with a glass packed with nutritious banana, apple, and spinach, you might just discover your own ninja power. Ka-pow!

INGREDIENTS

- 4 ice cubes
- 1 cup plain, unsweetened almond milk
- 2 tablespoons natural peanut or almond butter
- 1 banana, broken in half
- 1 medium sweet apple, cored and sliced
- 2 handfuls baby spinach

INSTRUCTIONS

1. Combine all the ingredients in a blender.
2. Blend it all together until the mixture is smooth and uniform in color.
3. Pour into glasses and enjoy.

Lighten It Up, **DUDE!**

MAKE SURE YOUR NATURAL PEANUT BUTTER CONTAINS ONLY NUTS—NO SALT OR OTHER ADDITIVES.

DID YOU KNOW, BRO?

IN NAPLES, ITALY, IN 2016, 100 CHEFS JOINED FORCES TO BREAK THE GUINNESS WORLD RECORD FOR THE LONGEST PIZZA EVER MADE. THE PIZZA WAS MORE THAN 1 MILE LONG AND WAS MADE USING 4,409 POUNDS OF FLOUR, 3,527 POUNDS OF TOMATOES, 4,409 POUNDS OF CHEESE, AND 211 QUARTS OF OLIVE OIL.

SWEET, DUDE!

CAN A NINJA EAT PIZZA FOR BREAKFAST, LUNCH, DINNER, AND DESSERT? MAYBE YES, MAYBE NO. EITHER WAY, YOU GOTTA TRY! GO ALL OUT WITH:

- BERRY AWESOME (PAGE 103)
- DOJO DELIGHT (PAGE 105)
- CASEY'S COOKIES (PAGE 107)
- YOGURT CRUNCH (PAGE 109)
- PEANUT-BUTTER-AND-JELLY JUSTICE (PAGE 110)
- SLICE OF THE ACTION PIZZA (PAGE 111)
- NEW YORK CHEESECAKE (PAGE 113)
- DONNIE'S CHOC-TATO CHIP EXPERIMENT (PAGE 114)
- NINJA STARS (PAGE 115)
- GIMME S'MORES! (PAGE 117)
- NICE CREAM PIZZA (PAGE 119)

OF COURSE, AS WITH ANY DESSERT, THESE TREATS AREN'T FOR EVERY DAY BUT INSTEAD SHOULD BE ENJOYED ON AWESOME OCCASIONS SUCH AS BIRTHDAYS, HOLIDAYS, AND SAVING THE PLANET FROM THE KRANG. SWEET!

BERRY AWESOME

MAKES 4
PERSONAL PIZZAS

Disappointed by the dinky micro pies they had at MacDonald Crump's Peek-A-Peck-O-Pizza, the Turtles made it their mission to create some seriously satisfying personal pizzas. Here's one of their favorites so far: individual pizza crusts slathered with lemony ricotta and topped with fresh blackberries, raspberries, and blueberries.

INGREDIENTS

Extra-virgin olive oil for greasing

1 ½ cups ricotta cheese

1 teaspoon lemon zest

1-pound ball pizza dough, homemade
   (pages 17-19) or store-bought

1 cup balsamic vinegar

2 tablespoons honey

½ pint fresh blackberries

½ pint fresh raspberries

1 pint fresh blueberries

4 teaspoons chopped fresh mint leaves

Lighten It Up,
DUDE!

USE WHOLE-WHEAT PIZZA
DOUGH (PAGE 18) AND
LOW-FAT RICOTTA.

INSTRUCTIONS

1. Place racks in the top and bottom thirds of your oven and preheat to 500°F. Rub two heavy-duty, rimmed baking sheets with a little olive oil.

2. In a small bowl, mix together the ricotta cheese and lemon zest.

3. Divide the pizza dough into four equal-size pieces and roll out each one to a 4-inch disk.

4. Place the dough disks on the prepared baking sheets and spread the ricotta cheese on top.

5. Bake for 6 to 8 minutes, switching the position of the baking sheets halfway through, until the crust is golden brown.

6. Remove the pizzas from the oven and set aside.

7. Meanwhile, combine the balsamic vinegar and honey in a medium saucepan over medium-high heat and bring the mixture to a boil. Let it boil for 7 to 10 minutes or until it looks like syrup.

8. Remove the pan from the heat and stir in the berries.

9. Top the pizzas with the berry mixture and garnish with the chopped mint. Serve immediately.

DOJO DELIGHT

MAKES ONE
12-INCH PIZZA

This pizza's got your fresh fruit serving covered, and it'll satisfy those after-dinner sweet cravings. Double bonus!

INGREDIENTS

- 1 sheet frozen puff pastry, thawed
- 1 cup plain Greek yogurt
- 2 tablespoons honey
- 1/2 teaspoon ground cinnamon
- 1/4 teaspoon pure vanilla extract
- 1 cup sliced pineapple
- 1 cup halved purple grapes
- 1 cup sliced kiwis, whole slices or half moons
- 1 cup sliced strawberries
- 1 tablespoon chopped fresh mint

INSTRUCTIONS

1. Preheat the oven to 400°F.
2. Place the pastry sheet on a floured work surface and roll it out to a 12-inch circle.
3. Place the pastry sheet on a pizza pan or heavy-duty, rimmed baking sheet. Prick it all over with the tines of a fork to prevent bubbling.
4. Bake for 10 to 15 minutes or until the pastry is golden in color.
5. Remove the pastry from the oven and place it on a wire rack to cool completely in the pan.
6. In a medium bowl, stir together the yogurt, honey, cinnamon, and vanilla.
7. When the crust has cooled to room temperature, spread the yogurt mixture evenly on top and press the fruit into the yogurt in the pattern of your choice.
8. Sprinkle with the mint, then slice and serve.

Lighten It Up, DUDE!

USE LOW-FAT PLAIN GREEK YOGURT.

CASEY'S COOKIES

MAKES 2 TO 3 DOZEN COOKIES

Casey Jones likes pizza just as much as the Turtles do—and he's totally down to prank his family and party guests with these pizza look-alikes! Here, the sugar cookies are topped with olives (black-tinted icing), pepperoni (cinnamon candies), and oregano (green sugar), but you can experiment with whatever pizza inventions you dream up.

INGREDIENTS

COOKIES

2 ½ cups all-purpose flour

½ teaspoon baking powder

½ teaspoon salt

2 sticks (1 cup) unsalted butter at room temperature

¾ cup sugar

1 large egg

1 teaspoon vanilla extract

TOPPINGS

1-pound box confectioners' sugar

2 large egg whites or 5 tablespoons meringue powder

½ cup water

Gel food coloring (red, yellow, blue, and black)

Red cinnamon candies

Green sprinkles or sugar

INSTRUCTIONS

TO MAKE THE COOKIES

1. In a medium bowl, whisk together the flour, baking powder, and salt.

2. In the bowl of an electric mixer fitted with the paddle attachment, beat together the butter and sugar for 3 to 5 minutes or until light and fluffy.

3. Add the egg and vanilla and beat just until incorporated.

4. Dump in the flour mixture and beat on low speed until everything is combined and the dough comes together.

5. Divide the dough in half. Plop half of the dough onto a sheet of plastic wrap and flatten it into a disk, then wrap it tightly. Repeat with the other half of dough.

6. Refrigerate the dough disks for at least 1 hour or up to 3 days. (Or, if you really like to plan ahead, make the dough and freeze it for up to 1 month. Then just move it to the fridge the night before you're ready to make cookies and let it defrost overnight.)

7. Arrange the racks in the top and bottom thirds of your oven and preheat to 350°F.

(continued on page 108)

8. On a floured work surface, roll out the dough to a ¼-inch thickness.

9. Punch out circle shapes using a 3-inch round cookie cutter or the rim of a glass. Reroll any scraps and cut out as many circles as you can.

10. Place the dough circles on two ungreased baking sheets, spacing them about 1 inch apart.

11. Bake for 10 to 15 minutes, switching the position of the baking sheets halfway through, until the cookies are light brown around the edges.

12. Remove the cookies from the oven and let them cool for about 5 minutes on the baking sheets, then transfer them to wire racks to cool completely.

TO MAKE THE ICING

1. Combine the sugar and egg whites or meringue powder in the bowl of an electric mixer fitted with the paddle attachment.

2. Beat on low speed until combined, then stream in ⅓ cup water.

3. Increase the speed to medium and beat until the mixture holds soft peaks when you lift the paddle (5 to 8 minutes). If the mixture seems too stiff, add more water, 1 tablespoon at a time, beating between additions until it reaches your desired consistency.

4. Set out four ramekins or small bowls. Spoon ¼ cup of the icing into one, ⅓ cup into another, ⅓ cup into another, and the rest into the last one. Tint the first one black, the second one red, and the third one light brown (7 drops red, 2 drops yellow, 1 drop blue). Leave the last one white. Cover the ramekins with plastic wrap while you work to prevent them from drying.

5. First, spoon little blobs of red icing ("sauce") onto each cookie and spread them evenly with the back of the spoon, leaving a ⅛- or ¼-inch border all around.

6. Next, scoop the light brown icing into a pastry bag (or resealable plastic bag with the tip of one bottom corner snipped off) and pipe it around each cookie to make the pizza crust. Let the sauce and crust dry.

7. Spoon a little dollop of white icing ("cheese") on each cookie and spread it out a little, making sure you don't cover the red "sauce" completely. Immediately press a few cinnamon candies ("pepperoni") onto each cookie.

8. When the white icing has dried, scoop the black icing into a pastry bag fitted with the smallest tip (or scoop it into a resealable plastic bag and snip off the very end of one bottom corner). Pipe little black olives onto each cookie and finish with a pinch of green sprinkles ("oregano").

9. Let the icing dry completely before serving.

YOGURT CRUNCH

MAKES ONE 12-INCH PIZZA

Flaky pastry crust, creamy yogurt, soft banana slices, and crunchy granola come together to form the perfect, sweet-but-not-too-sweet pizza for any time of day. If you don't have bananas on hand, substitute them with any other fruit you like.

INGREDIENTS

1 sheet frozen puff pastry, thawed

1 ½ cups vanilla Greek yogurt

2 bananas, sliced

½ cup granola

Lighten It Up, DUDE!

USE LOW-FAT VANILLA GREEK YOGURT AND ALL-NATURAL, WHOLE GRAIN GRANOLA.

INSTRUCTIONS

1. Preheat the oven to 400°F.

2. Place the pastry sheet on a floured work surface and roll it out to a 12-inch circle.

3. Place the dough on a pizza pan or heavy-duty, rimmed baking sheet. Prick it all over with the tines of a fork to prevent bubbling.

4. Bake for 15 to 20 minutes or until the pastry is golden in color. Remove the pastry from the oven and place it on a wire rack to cool completely in the pan.

5. When the crust has cooled to room temperature, spread the yogurt evenly on top and press the banana slices into the yogurt. Sprinkle with the granola. Slice and serve.

DID YOU KNOW, BRO?

OCTOBER WAS NAMED NATIONAL PIZZA MONTH IN 1984, AND IT IS STILL OBSERVED EVERY YEAR ACROSS THE UNITED STATES AND IN MANY PARTS OF CANADA.

PEANUT-BUTTER-AND-JELLY JUSTICE

MAKES 4 PERSONAL PIZZAS

Why hide peanut butter and jelly between two slices of boring old sandwich bread when you can enjoy them both on a still-warm pizza crust instead? Make some dough over the weekend and store it in the fridge, then whip up these personal snack pies whenever hunger strikes!

INGREDIENTS

Vegetable oil for greasing

1-pound ball pizza dough, homemade (pages 17-19) or store-bought

²/₃ cup natural peanut butter

¹/₃ cup fruit preserves

INSTRUCTIONS

1. Place racks in the top and bottom thirds of your oven and preheat to 450°F. Rub two heavy-duty, rimmed baking sheets with a little vegetable oil.

2. Divide the pizza dough into four equally sized pieces and roll out each one to a 4-inch disk.

3. Place the dough disks on the prepared baking sheets and bake them for 6 minutes or until they're just golden brown, switching the position of the baking sheets halfway through.

4. Remove them from the oven and set aside.

5. When the crusts have cooled a little, spread them with the peanut butter and then spoon the preserves on top.

6. Slice each pizza into squares or slices and serve.

Lighten It Up, DUDE!

USE WHOLE-WHEAT PIZZA DOUGH (PAGE 18) AND SUGAR-FREE FRUIT PRESERVES AND MAKE SURE THAT YOUR NATURAL PEANUT BUTTER CONTAINS ONLY NUTS—NO SALT OR OTHER ADDITIVES.

SLICE OF THE ACTION

MAKES 4 SERVINGS

Wait a minute. Pizza with no crust? This is really more like a fruit salad with pizza attitude. If you want to kick up the wow factor, throw the watermelon rounds on the grill for a few minutes before topping.

INGREDIENTS

1 large seedless watermelon

Fine sea salt

$\frac{1}{2}$ cup chopped, unsalted pistachio nuts

$\frac{1}{3}$ cup fresh pomegranate arils

1 cup fresh raspberries

Balsamic vinegar

4 teaspoons chopped fresh mint

INSTRUCTIONS

1. Cut four 1-inch-thick rounds from the widest part of the watermelon. Reserve the rest of the watermelon for another use.

2. Place the watermelon rounds on a few large cutting boards and season each with a small pinch of salt.

3. Top the "pizzas" with the pistachios, pomegranate, and raspberries, then drizzle each lightly with balsamic vinegar.

4. Finish with a sprinkle of mint. Slice and serve.

NEW YORK CHEESECAKE PIZZA

MAKES ONE 12-INCH PIZZA

What's more New York than strawberry cheesecake? How 'bout one you can eat with your hands? Make this one in late spring or early summer, when strawberries are at their freshest.

INGREDIENTS

CRUST

12 full graham cracker sheets, broken into pieces

6 tablespoons unsalted butter, melted

1/3 cup packed brown sugar

1/4 teaspoon salt

TOPPING

One 8-ounce package cream cheese at room temperature

1/2 cup plain Greek yogurt

1 tablespoon freshly squeezed lemon juice

2 tablespoons honey

1 teaspoon pure vanilla extract

1/8 teaspoon fine sea salt

2 cups thinly sliced fresh strawberries

1/4 cup low-sugar strawberry preserves

INSTRUCTIONS

TO MAKE THE CRUST

1. Place the graham crackers in the bowl of a food processor and grind them until they look like sand.

2. Add the butter, brown sugar, and salt, and pulse until combined.

3. Dump the mixture into a 12-inch pizza pan and press it out evenly, all the way to the edges. Use the bottom of a flat measuring cup to make sure it's as packed down as possible.

4. Refrigerate for at least 1 hour.

TO MAKE THE TOPPING

1. Place the cream cheese in the bowl of an electric mixer fitted with the whisk attachment.

2. Beat until fluffy, then add the yogurt, lemon juice, honey, vanilla, and salt. Beat until smooth.

3. Spread the cheesecake topping onto the crust.

4. Refrigerate for 24 hours or until the cheesecake is set.

5. Toss the strawberries with the preserves in a medium bowl, then spoon this mixture on top of the finished cheesecake. Slice and serve.

Lighten It Up, DUDE!

USE 100 PERCENT WHOLE-GRAIN GRAHAM CRACKERS, REDUCED-FAT CREAM CHEESE AND YOGURT, AND SUGAR-FREE STRAWBERRY PRESERVES.

DONNIE'S CHOC-TATO CHIP EXPERIMENT

MAKES ONE 12-INCH PIZZA

Donnie's always in his lab tinkering away until he comes up with something excellently unexpected! With this experiment, he learned that melted chocolate and potato chips are a match made in pizza heaven. One is smooth and the other is salty, and together they make one powerful team!

INGREDIENTS

Cornmeal or flour for dusting

Extra-virgin olive oil for greasing

1-pound ball pizza dough, homemade (pages 17-19) or store-bought

1 tablespoon unsalted butter, melted

1/2 cup chocolate-hazelnut spread

1/4 cup M&Ms

1/4 cup dark or semisweet chocolate chips

Small bag of plain, salted potato chips

Lighten It Up, DUDE!

USE WHOLE-WHEAT PIZZA DOUGH (PAGE 18) AND SKIP THE M&MS.

INSTRUCTIONS

BAKING STONE/STEEL: Place your baking stone on the middle rack of the oven and preheat to 500°F for at least 30 minutes. Dust a pizza peel or inverted baking sheet with cornmeal or flour.

BAKING SHEET: Preheat the oven to 500°F with a rack in the middle position. Lightly coat a heavy-duty, rimmed baking sheet with olive oil.

1. Stretch or roll the dough into a 12-inch disk and place it on the prepared pizza peel or baking sheet. Use your fingers to make dimples all over the dough. (This will prevent it from bubbling up in the oven.)

2. Brush the dough with the butter, then shimmy it from the peel to the hot baking stone or transfer the baking sheet to the oven.

3. Bake just until the crust is golden (5 to 7 minutes on the baking stone; 10 to 12 minutes on the baking sheet).

4. Remove the crust from the oven.

5. Scoop the chocolate-hazelnut spread onto the crust and smooth it out evenly using a spatula or the back of a spoon.

6. Top with the M&Ms, chocolate chips, and potato chips, and return the pizza to the oven.

7. Bake for about 2 minutes or until the chocolate just begins to melt.

8. Remove the pizza from the oven. Slice and serve.

NINJA STARS

MAKES 4
PERSONAL PIZZAS

Little ninjas can make these pizzas all on their own. Just toast the English muffins and lay them out on a work surface with the peanut butter and apple and kiwi slices within reach.

INGREDIENTS

2 English muffins, split

1/2 cup natural peanut butter

2 medium Granny Smith apples, peeled, cored, and very thinly sliced (you'll need 16 slices)

4 slices kiwifruit

INSTRUCTIONS

1. Toast the English muffins and spread some peanut butter on each half.

2. Arrange four apple slices on each English muffin half in the shape of a ninja star. Place a slice of kiwi in the center.

Lighten It Up, **DUDE!**

USE WHOLE-WHEAT ENGLISH MUFFINS AND MAKE SURE THAT YOUR NATURAL PEANUT BUTTER CONTAINS ONLY NUTS—NO SALT OR OTHER ADDITIVES.

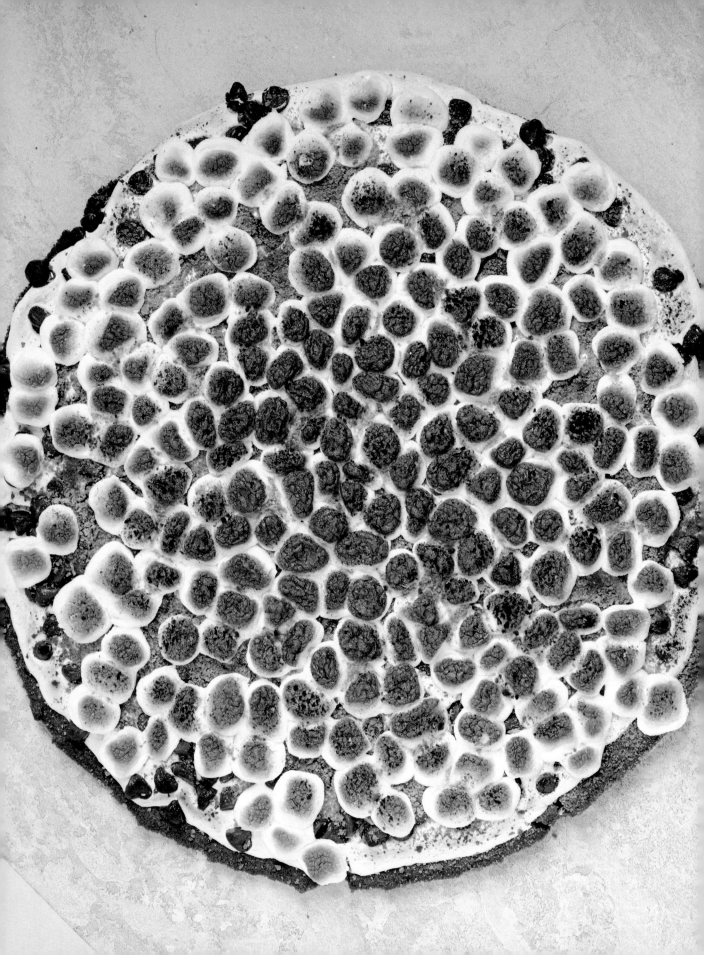

GIMME S'MORES!

MAKES ONE 12-INCH PIZZA

Few humans agree with the Turtles' love of marshmallow and guacamole pizza, but just about anyone can get behind this marshmallow and chocolate pizza with a graham cracker crust!

INGREDIENTS

CRUST

12 full graham cracker sheets, broken into pieces

6 tablespoons unsalted butter, melted

1/3 cup packed brown sugar

1/4 teaspoon salt

TOPPING

One 7-ounce container marshmallow cream

1 cup milk chocolate chips

1 full graham cracker sheet

1 1/2 cups mini marshmallows

USE 100 PERCENT WHOLE-GRAIN GRAHAM CRACKERS AND DARK OR SEMISWEET CHOCOLATE CHIPS AND CUT THE AMOUNT OF MINI MARSHMALLOWS IN HALF.

INSTRUCTIONS

TO MAKE THE CRUST

1. Set a rack in the top third of the oven. Preheat to 350°F.

2. Place the graham crackers in the bowl of a food processor and grind them until they look like sand.

3. Add the butter, brown sugar, and salt and pulse until combined.

4. Dump the mixture into a 12-inch pizza pan and press it out evenly all the way to the edges. Use the bottom of a flat measuring cup to make sure it's as packed down as possible.

5. Bake for 7 to 10 minutes or until the crust just begins to brown at the edges.

6. Remove the crust from the oven and let it cool for 5 minutes.

FOR ASSEMBLY

1. Spread the marshmallow cream on the cooled crust, then sprinkle the chocolate chips on top.

2. Bake for 10 minutes or until the chocolate has melted.

3. Meanwhile, place the graham cracker in a resealable plastic bag and pound it with a rolling pin until it resembles sand.

4. When the pizza is done baking, immediately remove it from the oven and turn on the broiler.

5. Scatter the mini marshmallows and graham cracker crumbs over the pizza and broil for 1 to 2 minutes or until the marshmallows are toasted.

6. Remove the pizza from the oven, let it cool for 5 minutes, then slice and serve.

NICE CREAM PIZZA

MAKES ONE 12-INCH PIZZA

Chocolate fudge is one of Mikey's favorite pizza toppings. If he had his way, he'd just eat it with sardines and chili peppers! But since he has to share with his bros, he's learned to pair the chocolate with ice cream and graham crackers for this surprisingly choice treat.

INGREDIENTS

12 full graham cracker sheets, broken into pieces

6 tablespoons unsalted butter, melted

1/3 cup packed brown sugar

1/4 teaspoon salt

1 pint vanilla ice cream, softened

Prepared chocolate fudge sauce, maraschino cherries, chopped fresh fruit, whipped cream, and anything else you like on ice cream sundaes

INSTRUCTIONS

1. Place the graham crackers in the bowl of a food processor and grind them until they look like sand.

2. Add the butter, brown sugar, and salt and pulse until combined.

3. Dump the mixture into a spring-form pan and press it out to cover the bottom of the pan.

4. Use your fingers or a flat-bottomed measuring cup to make sure it's as packed down as possible.

5. Refrigerate for at least 1 hour.

6. Spread the softened ice cream evenly over the chilled crust. Cover tightly with foil or plastic wrap, and freeze for at least 3 hours or overnight.

7. Remove the pizza from the pan. Pile on your favorite toppings. Slice and serve immediately.

Lighten It Up, DUDE!

USE 100 PERCENT WHOLE-GRAIN GRAHAM CRACKERS; REDUCED-FAT, LOW-SUGAR ICE CREAM; AND FRESH FRUIT FOR TOPPING.

PLANNING A TMNT PARTY

What's the best way to celebrate your favorite heroes in a half shell? Duh, dude—it's got to be a pizza party! Here are some tips and ideas to make it totally tubuloso.

INVITATIONS, DECORATIONS, AND FAVORS

- Create or purchase Teenage Mutant Ninja Turtles–themed invitations.

- Cut ninja masks out of blue, purple, red, and orange felt so guests can wear the color of their favorite Turtle.

- Use solid green tablecloths, with cups, plates, and napkins in the four colors of the Turtles.

- Make a pizza garland out of construction paper and string.

- Fill bowls with green candies and gummy worms or color-coordinate a wide range of candies and snacks in separate sections or small tables for Leonardo (blue), Donatello (purple), Raphael (red), and Michelangelo (orange).

FOOD IDEAS

- **Make-your-own-pizza bar:** Pre-bake a personal pizza crust for each guest and stack them on a platter. Arrange bowls of different sauces, shredded cheeses, and toppings on a large table (pizza sauce, pesto, cheddar, mozzarella, sliced olives, bell peppers, pineapple, ham, cooked bacon, pepperoni, and caramelized onions). Let each guest top their own pizza, then bake the pizzas in batches during the first activity.

- **Mikey's favorite pizzas:** Serve a few wacky pies such as Pepperoni and Sweet Pickle Pie (page 79), Pizza Portraits (page 58), and the Mac Attack (page 55).

- **Dessert pizzas:** Choose desserts that can be made ahead of time such as Casey's Cookies (page 107), New York Cheesecake Pizza (page 113), or Nice Cream Pizza (page 119).

ACTIVITIES FOR KIDS AND ADULTS

- **Coloring:** Buy coloring books or simply print black-and-white Turtle-face outlines. Cover a long table with a plastic tablecloth, set out a few big boxes of crayons, and let the creative juices flow!

- **The "Feed Michelangelo" beanbag toss:** Paste a large printout or poster of Mikey's face onto a piece of foam board and cut out his mouth. Take turns tossing small beanbags or cardboard pizza slices at the poster, keeping score as you go. Reward the person who ends up with the most points with a prize.

- **Shredder or Krang piñata:** Purchase or make a piñata in the shape of your favorite TMNT villain and fill it with all green or blue, purple, red, and orange candies. Hang it up outside or in the middle of a large room inside and let each micro-ninja take a swing or two with a plastic bat until the villain is defeated.

- **Pizza box relay race:** Set up two identical racecourses in the backyard (including obstacles for older kids). Divide the guests into two teams and give each team three to five empty pizza boxes. At the sound of the starting whistle, the first player from each team must balance the pizza boxes in one hand or on their head and race through the course. If the pizza boxes fall, they must stop and rebalance them before continuing on the course. When the first team member gets back to their team, they then give the boxes to the next team member. The winning team is the first to have all players complete the race.

BEVERAGES

- **Sewer water:** Fill a large, clear beverage dispenser with water, a few squeezes of lime, and a handful of torn mint leaves.

- **Green mutagen drinks:** Whip up a few batches of Green Ooze Smoothies (page 99) or serve pitchers of green sports drinks or green-tinted lemonade. For adults, make bright green cocktails like margaritas or mojitos.

MEASUREMENTS CONVERSION CHARTS

VOLUME

US	METRIC
⅕ teaspoon	1 ml
1 teaspoon	5 ml
1 tablespoon	15 ml
1 fluid ounce	30 ml
⅕ cup	50 ml
¼ cup	60 ml
⅓ cup	80 ml
3.4 fluid ounces	100 ml
½ cup	120 ml
⅔ cup	160 ml
¾ cup	180 ml
1 cup	240 ml
1 pint (2 cups)	480 ml
1 quart (4 cups)	.95 liter

WEIGHT

US	METRIC
0.5 ounce	14 grams
1 ounce	28 grams
¼ pound	13 grams
⅓ pound	151 grams
½ pound	227 grams
1 pound	454 grams

TEMPERATURE

FAHRENHEIT	CELSIUS
200°	93.3°
212°	100°
250°	121°
275°	135°
300°	149°
325°	165°
350°	177°
400°	205°
425°	220°
450°	233°
475°	245°
500°	260°

CONCLUSION

It seems we have come to the end of your ninja training. After working your way through this book—starting with the basics, moving up to classic pies, and then graduating to radical pizza mash-ups—you are now ready to embark on your own unique adventures, creating edible masterpieces that only you can imagine.

Master Splinter once said, "The path that leads to what we truly desire is long and difficult, but only by following that path do we achieve our goal."

Sometimes all the path entails is spreading sauce on a round of dough, topping it with whatever your heart desires, and baking it in the oven. Go forth, young warriors. Party on, make pies, and cowabunga!

ABOUT THE AUTHOR & PHOTOGRAPHER

Peggy Paul Casella is a cookbook writer and editor and the creator of ThursdayNightPizza.com, a food blog centered on making weekly pizzas from scratch. In her editing and writing life, she wrangles hundreds—sometimes thousands—of recipes each month from chefs, writers, and publishers all over the country; writes a regular column on seasonal produce for a local Philadelphia magazine; and contributes sporadically to other publications. Peggy started Thursday Night Pizza in 2014 as a way to play with seasonal ingredients and test out all sorts of weird and wonderful flavor combinations, mad scientist style. She grew up watching the original Teenage Mutant Ninja Turtles cartoon and considers Michelangelo a true pizza visionary. She lives in Philadelphia, PA.

Albert Yee is a professional photographer and devoted lover of food, particularly pizza. Upon moving from New York to his adopted home of Philadelphia, he promptly went on a frenzied taste test of twenty or so pizza shops to find a new "home slice" to enjoy. When not eating a slice, he can be found photographing some part of the mid-Atlantic region's food economy, whether it be on a farm, at a restaurant, or in a market. He now lives blocks away from the nation's first and only pizza museum and what many have come to consider the country's best pizza pie. He lives in Philadelphia, PA.

AUTHOR ACKNOWLEDGMENTS

Thanks to my husband, John, for your endless encouragement; for being my go-to taste-tester, dishwasher, and tech support; and for humoring me as I binge-watched TMNT cartoons for three months straight and brainstormed my way through some pretty bodacious pizza concoctions.

Thanks to Gretchen and Corey for helping me get where I am today; to Nathan and Daphne for keeping me in touch with my inner kid; to Chris, the custodian of knowledge, for your TMNT subject-matter expertise; to Anne for lending me your crafting brain; to everyone who agreed to come over on recipe testing days without knowing what you'd be eating; and to all my family and friends—especially Scott and Thea—who supported me from the very beginning of my pizza journey.

Mondo kudos to Albert Yee for transforming my tiny kitchen into a legit photography studio and making even the wackiest pies look totally tubuloso. We make a great team, dude!

To Clare Pelino, thanks for taking a chance on me! To my editor, Kelly Reed, and everyone at Insight Editions, including Elaine Ou, Chrissy Kwasnik, Brie Brewer, and Katie DeSandro, thanks for your direction, creativity, and undeniable Turtle power. Big thanks to the folks at Nickelodeon, too, especially Raina Moore.

As Master Splinter once said, "Together, there is nothing [you] cannot accomplish. Help each other, draw upon one another, and always remember the power that binds you."

PHOTOGRAPHER ACKNOWLEDGMENTS

I'd like to thank my wife, Katie Donnelly, for always believing in me and my abilities no matter the project or obstacle in front of me. She has always encouraged and pushed me forward along the way and has been my bulwark when I've needed it. I'd like to thank Peggy for her indefatigable spirit during this fun collaboration we took on together. We spent many hot summer days together by her oven, which fired up recipe after recipe for this book.

INSIGHT
EDITIONS

www.insighteditions.com

Find us on Facebook: www.facebook.com/InsightEditions

Follow us on Instagram: @insighteditions

nickelodeon

Published by Insight Editions, San Rafael, California, in 2017.

Library of Congress Cataloging-in-Publication Data available.

ISBN: 978-1-60887-831-4

Publisher: Raoul Goff
Art Director: Chrissy Kwasnik
Designer: Brie Brewer
Executive Editor: Vanessa Lopez
Project Editor: Kelly Reed
Associate Editor: Katie DeSandro
Managing Editor: Alan Kaplan
Production Editor: Elaine Ou
Production Manager: Alix Nicholaeff
Production Assistant: Sylvester Vang

 ROOTS of PEACE  REPLANTED PAPER

Insight Editions, in association with Roots of Peace, will plant two trees
for each tree used in the manufacturing of this book. Roots of Peace is
an internationally renowned humanitarian organization dedicated to
eradicating land mines worldwide and converting war-torn lands into
productive farms and wildlife habitats. Roots of Peace will plant two
million fruit and nut trees in Afghanistan and provide farmers there with
the skills and support necessary for sustainable land use.

Manufactured in China by Insight Editions

20 19 18 17 16 15 14 13 12